D1795945

THE AUDACITY TO TEACH!

The Impact of Leadership, School Reform, and the Urban Context on Educational Innovations

---

Jacob Easley II

University Press of America,® Inc.
Lanham · Boulder · New York · Toronto · Plymouth, UK

Contents

Foreword

Urban education during the last two decades has been heavily influenced by political and economic pressures for reform. With student achievement lagging in general and the racial achievement gap growing, many, including former Secretary of Education Rod Paige, are calling improving educational outcomes for students in our nation's urban schools the greatest civil rights issue of our time.

With passage of the No Child Left Behind Act in January, 2002, the success of students, schools, and school districts has been tied to the attainment of Adequate Yearly Progress (AYP). Failure to attain AYP has resulted in sanctions being leveled at schools ranging from restricting the use of federal funds to reconstitution or school closure.

With the election of Barack Obama, a new sense of direction is emerging with respect to educational reform in our urban schools. The President's view of reform, as articulated by Secretary of Education Arne Duncan, focuses on improving teacher quality, support for new service delivery systems, and better use of student achievement data to inform and improve instructional practice.

Dr. Jacob Easley II provides a concise and compelling overview of the dichotomy that exists between compliance with federal requirements associated with school improvement and the instructional practices and strategies that when employed correctly and consistently, elevate student achievement. Throughout his book *The Audacity to Teach!*, Dr. Easley provides a comprehensive overview of theories that influence the logistics of school reform, that is, why certain strategies are chosen. Dr. Easley also captures what the intended outcomes for reform can be if these strategies are implemented with a high degree of reconciled sensitivity to both the tenets of reform and the context of schools.

Dr. Easley has also crafted a view of the role of the practitioner with respect to school reform. If one accepts Dr. Easley's premise that the success or failure of efforts to elevate achievement are determined by the willingness of instructional staff to accept and utilize the various reform strategies presented to them, it will be invaluable for the reader to learn via first-hand accounts from teachers the substance of the challenges and opportunities for teachers to inform and improve their practice as a way to increase student achievement.

Urban schools, such as the one depicted in *The Audacity to Teach!*, can provide a high quality educational experience for students. There are countless numbers of schools serving poor, minority children across this country that are thriving academically. Learning how these schools have implemented practices which enable them to grow and sustain achievement is of the utmost importance.

This is particularly true as we move away from attaining a high school diploma as a minimum educational goal to demonstrating college readiness in mathematics, science, language arts, and social studies.

As a superintendent of schools who has worked primarily in schools and school districts serving poor, minority students, informing those who currently work in or desire to work in an urban setting of the intricacies and rewards of serving this population is vitally important. It is my hope that those reading *The Audacity to Teach!* will recognize that what represents audacity is not one's physical presence in an urban school or providing service to those who are deemed to be "at-risk". Audacity will be characterized by bold, innovative, collaborative, student focused, and compassionate administration and instruction. This instruction will challenge students in a way that affirms their ability to learn and succeed and deepen the students' desire to learn and succeed more. Educators can meet the challenges of this student population and serve them well. It is our collective professional responsibility to do so.

Dr. Bernard Taylor Jr.
Superintendent, Grand Rapids Public Schools, Michigan

Acknowledgements

I would like to thank the teachers, staff, and principals of Hillside Elementary School for opening their offices, classrooms, and work space to talk with me and to share their deepest insights about the conditions of education reform and schooling. Their participation and candid expressions serve to remind us of the hard work that goes on in schools, but more importantly their dedication to the students of Hillside is to be recognized by all. I would also like to thank my mentor, Daniel (Dan) Marshall for continuous feedback and encouragement.

Many family members and friends were an invaluable support during the data collection and writing of this book. My mother, Delois Lee, and friends Drs. Jean-Philippe Marelli and Trevor Brown, and Dott. Federico Ferrari were invaluable as critical listeners and reviewers.

In memoriam, this book is dedicated to my father Jacob Easley and my grandparents Katherine Daniels, Jennie Mae Easley, and Leon Easley.

Introduction

We must also challenge the system that prevents us from promoting and re-warding excellence in teaching. We cannot ask our teachers to perform the im-possible–to teach poorly prepared children with inadequate resources, and then punish them when children perform poorly on a standardized test. But if we give teachers the resources they need; if we pay them more, and give them time for professional development; if they are given ownership over the design of better assessment tools and a creative curricula; if we shape reforms with teachers rather than imposing changes on teachers, then it is fair to expect bet-ter results. Where there are teachers who are still struggling and underperform-ing, we should provide them with individual help and support.

Barack Obama, June 16, 2008

Capacity: The Nexus between Teaching and Learning

Prior to the election of President Obama in 2008 and even prior to the 2001 reauthorization of the Federal Elementary and Secondary Education Act (ESEA) under his predecessor President George W. Bush, one principal of an urban elementary school also held strong beliefs about the potential of rethinking education as usual. As the leader hired to turn around a chronically underper-forming school, he believed in the power of quality teaching and learning for the academic advancement of one of America's poorest, minority student popula-tions. This principal believed that in order for school reconstitution to yield success toward school improvement, the staff development programming, work-ing relations among teachers, and instructional practices would have to be reconceptualized in a particular way. Mr. Thachery's[1] beliefs were intricately linked to the notion that particular strategies are needed for increasing teacher quality and for unraveling ineffective teaching and learning practices. For example, during the processes of staffing a new faculty, he actively sought to hire teachers who "would be receptive to what may have been perceived to be unconventional ways of teaching in the elementary environment" and within an urban context (personal communication, April 3, 2003). Because of this princip-al's high regard for capacity building for quality teaching and learning, as well as the unique context of school reconstitution and subsequent, serial reforms, this book focuses on the conditions of compounding school change and its impact on teachers' capacity for engaging in teaching and learning innovations.

Related research (Little, 2001; Lieberman, 1996; Malen et al., 2002) has shown that policy-driven reform as well as professional development agendas aimed at building the capacity for quality teaching and learning practices bring about a fair amount of stress in the daily work lives of teachers. These stresses make the promise of reforms unstable, particularly as related to the reforms' ability to build the capacity for teacher quality and excellence in teaching and learning. In other words, reform can oftentimes roll out as a double-edged sword, one that is as likely to build capacity as it is to dismantle it. While a paucity of research has focused on the theory-of-action that guides reconstitution and the reform's effects on the working lives of educators, research in this area is limited (Malen et al., 2002). A small body of research explores issues of social and human capital regarding reconstitution (Rice & Croninger, 2001; Rice & Malen, 2002); yet this research is primarily limited to the intensification of the reform as explained through social norms and resource alignment. More specifically, studies that address the notions of capacity for teaching and learning as existing within, derived from, and/or shaped by the context of reconstitution is sparse and underdeveloped, at best.

This is not to mention research that expands the understandings of the effects of incessant school change on the capacity for teachers' engagement in teaching and learning innovations is paramount to inform policy and practices for creating the educational conditions of possibility espoused by Mr. Thachery and echoed by President Obama. In addition, these understandings are inextricable from the examination of teachers' knowledge use (i.e., their actualized capacity for teaching and learning innovations), which remains underdeveloped as well. Wideen, Mayer-Smith, and Moon (1996) contend that, "Despite . . . interest in knowledge utilization in the social sciences, researchers in education have not dealt with the issue of professional knowledge [i.e, teachers' contemplations about their capacity] and the way teachers use it to inform their [teaching and learning] practices" (p. 187).

This book is developed from the study of an inner-city, urban elementary school that has undergone serial school reforms. One of these is reconstitution, a drastic comprehensive school reform approach in which incumbent teachers and administrators in a chronic, low-performing school are replaced with new faculty and leadership in the hope of spurring new working conditions and raising student achievement. The student population, however, remains the same. Another is the 2001 Federal, No Child Left Behind Act (NCLB) and its embedded, multidimensional standards and accountability policies that have impacted curriculum and instruction. Others include curricular changes, along with leadership turnover. Each act of reform has promised to improve this particular school. A significant measure for improvement has been and continues to be the results of students' performance on some sort of standardized assessment. The implementation of serial comprehensive reforms, as well as the high-stakes accountability pressures of NCLB, has shaped the context of schooling within this site. More importantly, these are the working conditions that inform teachers' actualized capacity for engagement in teaching and learning innovations aimed to foster student success.

This book is derived from the axiom that the core of education exists at the classroom level and is represented by the teaching and learning processes that is mediated through relationships between teachers and their students. Teachers, however, hold particular interpretations about the extent to which serial comprehensive reforms affect their capacity for innovation within the teaching and learning process. This book explores these interpretations through an examination of the lived experience of teachers who seek to improve the academic achievement and success of their students. The primary data collection strategies are in-depth interviews and classroom observations that focus on teachers' collective definition of teaching and learning innovations for increasing student learning. Participating teachers represent a continuum of years of experience in classrooms as well as their development in innovative teaching. Yet, they each describe, talk about, and demonstrate how the context of serial comprehensive school reform shaped their capacity to engage in teaching and learning innovations. While some contemplations are individual, others are shared among members. One position shared among teachers is that their engagement in teaching and learning innovations is aimed to improve students' learning and levels of academic success.

The examination of students' actual learning and academic achievement is not addressed, as such attention would require a different set of guiding questions and a different research design. Indeed, the direct impact of teaching and learning innovations on students' success is important. Yet, the means by which such instructional innovations are made possible are equally critical.

The details of teachers' experiences in this book affirm the idea of an educational core for teaching and learning and demonstrate that teachers' capacity for innovation within this core is influenced by broader educational decisions and conditions stretching from beyond the classroom level. Such findings highlight the reality that schools exist within and are responsive to larger sociopolitical systems such as school districts and local communities (Sarason, 1990; Noguera, 2003; Lipman, 1998). As a result, capacity is made complex, evolving from multiple levels (e.g., national, state, local, and school building levels). Because the complexities of capacity directly affect teachers' instructional innovations and, in turn, their teaching influences students' learning, capacity becomes the nexus between teaching and learning. Capacity, in this regard, is the engine for those with the audacity to teach.

Notes

1. The names are pseudonyms to protect the anonymity of school leaders and faculty.

Chapter One
The Contemporary Context of Urban Schools

In 1983, the National Commission on Excellence in Education released *A Nation at Risk*. This report brought to the forefront of contemporary American politics the need to seriously focus on the improvement of schools. Goodlad (1984) supported the report's claims by declaring that "American schools are in trouble" (p. 1). A national assault on the failure of American schools ensued. Yet, nine years later, Finn (1992) explained that many American parents have continually expressed an approval of their own children's education and their local schools. He further clarified, however, that such approval ratings tend to be more true for certain schools than others. That is, many middle and upper class families have been able to maintain the sentiment that "The nation may be at risk, but 'I'm all right, Jack'" (Finn, 1992, p. xii). Thus, the prognosis of *A Nation at Risk* can be better understood by reconceptualizing American education as existing within the context of two American school systems. Preceding "A Nation at Risk" by more than 22 years, Conant (1961) referred to these two American schools systems as metropolitan slums and their suburbs. Following this logic, schools may be divided along class lines to include those that serve "secure" families and those that serve families "placed at-risk" economically, socially, politically, and otherwise. In this regard, the reform of American schools may be more accurately couched as a reform of the socioeconomically impoverished schools typically described as "inner-city," urban schools. These schools, not to exclude similar conditions faced by impoverished rural schools, stand in stark contrast to their suburban and more (economically) stable metropolitan (not classified as inner-city) counterparts.

For generations, inner-city, urban schools serving large numbers of minority students have been categorically and endlessly labeled inferior to suburban White schools. The gauge has been students' scores on standardized tests as well as other markers including grade point averages, high school graduation rates, and post secondary matriculation volumes. For example, standardized test scores have been used as the primary source for the following analyses about student achievement and the quality of instruction in inner-city, high poverty, and minority populated schools: compared to their suburban counterparts, students in urban schools, particularly urban high poverty schools, face greater challenges to overcome regarding student achievement (NCES, 1996); and the lowest levels of student achievement come from the 25 largest (urban) metropolitan school districts which educate approximately one fourth of the nation's African American students and one third of the Nation's Hispanic students (Education

Week/Pew Charitable Trust, 1998; Orfield & Eaton, 1996). Furthermore, the U.S. achievement gap between Asian and White students, combined, and Latino students is on par with the score gap between the U.S. and the highest performing counties on the Program in International Student Assessment (Stage, 2005).

Offering a gentle critique of the nation's attention to school reform, Meier (2002) explains that, "We are witnessing a radical redefinition of the task of public education, driven by the widespread belief that by focusing our attention on externally imposed tests we can both produce higher [student] achievement and restore public trust in our schools [, particularly urban schools]" (p. 95). In reaction to such analyses, a myriad of reform models have been proposed and initiated in order to improve schools. More specifically, the language of school improvement is often inextricable from that of reform, and reform (whether originating externally or from within schools) is often the context for school improvement. Moreover, reform (e.g., site based management, charter schools, class size reduction, character education, etc.) has come to be known as the tool of/for school improvement. Hence, the belief prevails that in the absence of reform, school improvement is compromised. The need for inner-city, urban school reform has come to shape the language, policy, and research of educational stakeholders who seek to discover the technologies needed to improve the function of schools as measured by student achievement outcomes. Yet, while reform has become commonplace in the education arena, particularly for urban schools, the anticipated outcomes for large scale improvement have yet to follow.

The Context of Reform Policy and Teaching and Learning

Since the publication of *A Nation at Risk*, national attention toward school improvement and the rate of policy enactments making way for many comprehensive reform models (e.g. Success for All, America's Choice, The Accelerated School Project, etc.) have gained momentum. For example, Leonard Haynes, Special Assistant, Office of the Secretary, United States Department of Education (personal communication, July 18, 2002) explains that because of the 2001 reauthorization of The Elementary and Secondary Education Act (commonly known as President Bush's No Child Left Behind Act), education and educational change have moved to the forefront of conversations among the broader American (U.S.) public. This growing, public interest in school reform developed at a rate tantamount to that which contemporary political leaders have been able to gain voter support by advancing the notion that America's schools are in a state of decline. Stated more precisely, the growing interest in public education from political figureheads has greatly influenced the ideology around school failure and the language of school reform. For example, Goodlad (2002) explains that Present Reagan's interest in the topic ensued only after being convinced of the "political mileage to be gained from promoting school reform" and that, in contemporary times, "The trick is to keep alive and well the message that our schools are failing" (p. 18). This message has and continues to ignite political interest in school reform, particularly for inner-city, urban schools defined by low test scores, large populations of minority and Limited English Proficient (LEP) learners, and low income families. And, each administration's (re)authorization of federal educational policies suggests that its executive authors have the solution for improving schools and increasing student achievement by fixing the problem at its core—inside the classroom where teaching and learning occur. This assessment is not offered to diminish the need for quality education and the importance of high levels of learning for all students. However, the fact cannot be ignored that education and educational improvement have become a highly politicized platform.

The primary strategy at the federal level has been to build capacity for change through policy actions that create funding streams and data reporting reservoirs. For example, the federal government has defined teacher quality from a policy perspective, thereby creating a particular language and a particular reference for conceptualizing the factors that define what effective classroom practices might look like. As a result of the 1998 reauthorization of Title II accountability provisions of the Higher Education Act, the Secretary of Education is required to issue annual reports to Congress on the state of teacher quality nationwide (U.S. Department of Education, 2002b). This report is known as *The Secretary's Annual Report on Teacher Quality* and focuses on certification and licensure for pre-service and in-service teachers. This report, along with many others associated with NCLB, has linked school reform and school improvement to the notion of teacher quality. *The Secretary's Annual Report on Teacher Quality* (U.S. Department of Education, 2002b) contends that, "In order to leave no child behind, we need a highly qualified teacher in every classroom" (p. viii). Yet, at the federal level, quality is currently defined in limited terms around a teachers' attainment of college degrees and professional certification in their respective content area(s) of instruction; although, a new movement is afoot to correlate teacher quality with student learning outcome data, namely standardized test scores.

Aimed at practicing teachers, professional development is commonly recognized as the capacity source for supporting, improving, and sustaining teacher quality. Without question and supported by research, "Professional development is considered an essential mechanism for deepening teachers' content knowledge and developing their teaching practices" (Desimone, Porter, Garet, Yoon, & Birman, 2002, p. 81). Therefore, professional development aimed at deepening teachers' content knowledge and developing their teaching practices simultaneously supports reform efforts to improve schools by enhancing what Prestine and McGreal (1997) call the core technology of schools. For example, the impact of professional development on student learning has been cited in research like that of Harris and Sass (2007) who found that students learn more during a course of a year when their teacher has engaged in content focused professional development.

The core technology or educational core (Resnick & Hall, 1998) of schooling is commonly thought of as the correspondence between teaching (i.e. teachers' instructional practices) and learning (i.e. student learning and student achievement). Thus, the essence of student achievement occurs as a result of the core technology of schooling, in the classroom, and through a relationship that suggests that teachers' instructional capacities and the quality of their classroom practices have a direct effect on students' learning. Hence, the theoretical and practical positions of policy driven school reform, teacher quality, and teaching and learning converge. This point of convergence is conceptualized as the viable means for school improvement; the efficacy of this convergence is commonly measured by the rise or fall of student achievement.

The growing role of federal policy is an important consideration in the examination of large-scale efforts to build capacity for the improvement of schools, primarily at the school's core. Yet, the impact of this growing role is felt at all areas of the school workplace. This is particularly true for inner-city, urban schools. For example, NCLB's Title I impacts the funding for school reform options designed to serve high poverty and minority populations; Title III impacts the ways in which schools address the needs of Limited English Proficient students; and Title II influences the ways in which states, school districts, and schools of education approach teacher quality. As schools make changes to meet the required regulations for compliance upon the receipt of federal reform dollars, policy directly shapes the context of school improvement and the context of teaching and learning.

Reconstitution, for example, is understood as a policy driven, comprehensive school reform option for school improvement available to states and school districts. Reconstitution is also formally recognized by NCLB as a viable comprehensive reform model approved for financial support at the federal level. Reconstitution shapes the context of schools by seeking to remove incumbent teaching, administrative and support staff for the purpose of starting the next school year with a new personnel composition (in whole or in part). The student population, however, is left intact. School reconstitution is considered by some to be the most drastic form of comprehensive school reform, and has historically occurred only in urban—low income and minority populated—schools (National Education Association, 1998) beginning with the San Francisco Unified School District in 1983 (Goldstein, Kelemen, & Koski, 1998). The aim of reconstitution is to increase a school's capacity for quality teaching and learning by re-staffing the school with more committed educators (Malen, Croninger, Redmond, & Muncey, 1999; Malen, Croninger, Muncey, & Redmond-Jones, 2002; Jones & Malen, 2002).

Though research has produced less than a handful of published studies on reconstitution, the trend has been for states and districts to support the capacity for quality teaching and learning by offering additional financial support to reconstituted schools for staff development programming (Goldstein et al., 1998; Borman, Rachuba, Datnow, Alberg, MacIver, Stringfield, & Ross 2000; Malen et al., 2002). Similarly, NCLB earmarks federal monies to support the improvement of student achievement through high quality and continuous staff development and the recruitment and retention of highly qualified core subject teachers. These policy driven, monetary provisions are significant in view of political platforms that make claims about the inferiority of public schools and the need for a high quality teaching force. These monetary provisions serve as a capacity source for school reform and improvement, particularly in support of improving the school's core where teaching and learning occurs.

Capacity for the Engagement in Teaching and Learning Innovations

The purpose of this book is to discuss the relationships between teachers' contemplations, that is, their thoughts, beliefs, reflections, and feelings about pedagogical capacity and their engagement in teaching and learning innovations within the context of an urban reconstituted school. As a researcher working closely with teachers in their school, I applied the following question to guide my observations of classroom practices as well as my dialogues with teachers: Within an urban reconstituted school that has faced subsequent and compounding reforms, what relationships, if any, do teachers perceive between their individual and collective pedagogical capacity and their engagement in teaching and learning innovations? This question gets as the heart of what many policy reform initiatives, school leaders, education researchers, and even teachers find central to school effectiveness and improvement. For failing urban schools, this question is of paramount importance; that is, an understanding of the conditions that directly impact the quality of education at its core, in the classroom, is vital for making inroads toward unearthing the essential means for unsettling a system that asks teachers to perform the impossible with inadequate conditions and resources, and within a context of serial reform.

Definitions: The Language of Reform, Capacity, and Engagement

School reconstitution, pedagogical capacity for teacher engagement, and the notion of teachers' engagement in teaching and learning innovations are defined in particular ways. The following definitions and conceptual diagram (see Figure A.) seek to demonstrate the interconnectedness among these constructs.

Reconstitution
Reconstitution is defined as a policy-based comprehensive school reform strategy aimed at improving schools. Reconstitution involves removing incumbent administrators, teachers and staff (in part, if not in whole) and replacing them

with more capable and committed educators (Malen et al., 1999; Malen, et al., 2002).

Reconstitution was first enacted as a policy decision to turn around low-performing schools in San Francisco, CA. In 1983, the San Francisco Unified School District (SFUSD) was court ordered into a Consent Decree with the San Francisco chapter of the National Association for the Advancement of Colored People (NAACP). Since the onset of reconstitution in the SFUSD, many other school districts have implemented reconstitution in some form: Chicago, Baltimore, and Atlanta for example.

Comprehensive School Reform

In 1998, the Comprehensive School Reform Program (CSR) was authorized under Title I, Part F of NCLB. The purpose of CSR is:

> to improve student achievement by supporting the implementation of comprehensive school reforms based on scientifically-based research and effective practices so that all children, especially those in low-performing, high poverty schools, can meet challenging State content and academic achievement standards. (U.S. Department of Education, 2002, p. 1)

This program is guided by the theory-of-action that espouses the need to bring together unified, coherent, and integrated strategies for school improvement in a way in which strategies are not isolated, are comprehensive, and are complimentary. This premise supports Fullan's (2001b) explanation that many simultaneously implemented school reform efforts fail because they incite change overload. Furthermore, comprehensive reform, according to CSR (U.S. Department of Education, 2002), seeks to address reform among elements that are important to the daily life of schools: strong academic content and research-based strategies; measurable goals; support by and for staff; professional development; parental involvement; technical assistance; evaluation; and the allocation of resources, brought together in an integrated, comprehensive way (p. 1).

While the CSR provides a framework for comprehensive school reform defined by the above elements, the program makes only sketchy recommendations regarding structural changes (or locus of change) within schools as an integral part of such reform. Furthermore, while the program offers financial assistance to state educational agencies (SEAs) for distribution to local education agencies (LEAs) to fund schools identified for improvement or corrective action, CSR makes no recommendations toward any particular program by name. However, the At-Risk Institute (formally known as the National Institute on Education of At-Risk Students) has divided programs into three primary categories according to the models' locus of change toward comprehensive school reform. These are: (1) models that focus on changing the organizational climate as well as classroom instruction, (2) models that focus on the classroom and/or curriculum by changing classroom management, instruction or curriculum, and (3) models that focus on professional development reform in order to strengthen the knowledge and skills of teachers and other staff working to serve large numbers of students placed at-risk for educational failure (U.S. Department of Education, 1998). CSR models may occur throughout a school, vertically across grade level units, for example, or vertically throughout a single grade level.

CSR models such as Success for All and the Accelerated Schools Projects can be found in most major U.S. public school districts. CSR, as a policy-supported remedy to low performing schools, gained momentum during the 1990s and through the early part of the 21st century. However, this approach to school reform lost much of its luster in the advent of debates to reauthorize NCLB under President Obama's administration. While the terms "comprehensive" and "school-wide" reform are often used interchangeably, within this book, comprehensive school reform is used in order to avoid ambiguity. Also, CSR is to refer to both the federal program as well as the concept of "comprehensive school reform" as implement at the SEA and LEA levels.

Pedagogical Capacity

Pedagogical capacity is defined as the critical conditions (e.g., political, social, ideological, and economic) that deny or grant, impede or support, and influence the potential for teachers to engage in the formal and informal processes of schooling.

Pedagogical capacity recognizes the conditions that define schools as dynamic systems of individuals undergoing change—systems that exist within larger social systems (Sarason, 1990). All schools undergoing change exist within and are influenced by districts. Simultaneously, district policies are influenced by agendas at the local, state, and federal levels. And, each of these echelons imposes its' own agenda(s) that are mediated through social, political, and economic conditions.

"Pedagogy," in this context, does not reference teaching practices alone, but acknowledges schools as existing within the above conditions (political, social, and economic) that work in complex ways. Pedagogy, within this context, is defined as "both a political and practical activity" that "attempts to influence the occurrences and qualities of experiences [in schools]" (Giroux & Simon, 1989, p. 222). In this context, pedagogy is simultaneously derived from a radical critique and critical discourse that recognizes, examines, and troubles schools as sites "tied to educational policy, interests, and resources that bear the weight of the logic and institutions of capitalism [at least here in the United States], [and] they also provide room for emancipatory teaching, knowledge, and social practices" (Giroux, 1983, p. 115). While the capacity is commonly understood as "the ability/potential to do something," Newmann, King, and Youngs (2001) contend that capacity refers to the "potential of material, a product, person, or group to fulfill a function if it is used in a particular [intended and deliberate] way" (p. 261). It then follows that the pedagogical capacity for teachers to engage in teaching and learning innovations is situational, complex, and is mediated by the myriad and lattice of interests, resources, and educational practices both within and outside of the school.

Engagement in Teaching and Learning Innovations

Engagement in efforts that yield teaching and learning innovations is defined as the acts of teachers' participation in and implementation of the formal and informal activities that they identify as "innovative teaching." This definition is derived from Wegner's (1998) work, which defines participation and engagement in a circular fashion. In this regard and in order for people to participate in social interactions, they must agree to mutual engagement. Wegner classifies participation as both a personal and social process that combines "doing, talking, thinking, feeling, and belonging" (p. 56). The teachers in this book unanimously (see Chapter Three) define teaching and learning innovations as practices that support students' learning. Their engagement in teaching and learning innovations exemplifies both the observable actions of doing and talking as well as the mental activities of thinking, feeling, and reflecting upon one's work for meaning making. Both are important for understanding the full range of teachers' knowledge use as they seek to promote student success.

While teachers' practices are often considered pedagogical practices, these are influenced by the broader notion of pedagogical capacities. Teachers' engagement in teaching and learning innovations is directly affected by their pedagogical capacity, that is, the social, political, economic, and intellectual means for engagement. For example, a particular teacher may express the desire to learn more about new reading strategies that have not been introduced in his or her school district. This teacher would need the pedagogical capacity to attend a conference, purchase literature and resources, and the time to practice and to reflect upon the results of his or her new skills. However, the relationships between teachers' pedagogical capacity and their engagement in teaching and learning innovations may prove to be dynamic within the context of a high-stakes reform. For instance, the working conditions of the teachers you will read about later are defined by a reconstituted school where one principal believed in the need to reconceptualize teachers' working relations due to the complex nature of reconstitution. Since this principal believed strongly in the need to rethink and redesign working norms to meet the particular goals of school reform, teachers' pedagogical capacity for engagement would have also needed to be rethought and redesigned. Here again, teachers' engagement in teaching and learning innovations is directly influenced by their pedagogical capacity for engagement.

While Figure A. suggests certain factors that might influence teachers' understandings about their pedagogical capacity to engage in teaching and learning innovations, these factors and others are contingent upon an examination of the lives of real teachers in a real school undergoing serial school reform. This book seeks to explore these complexities.

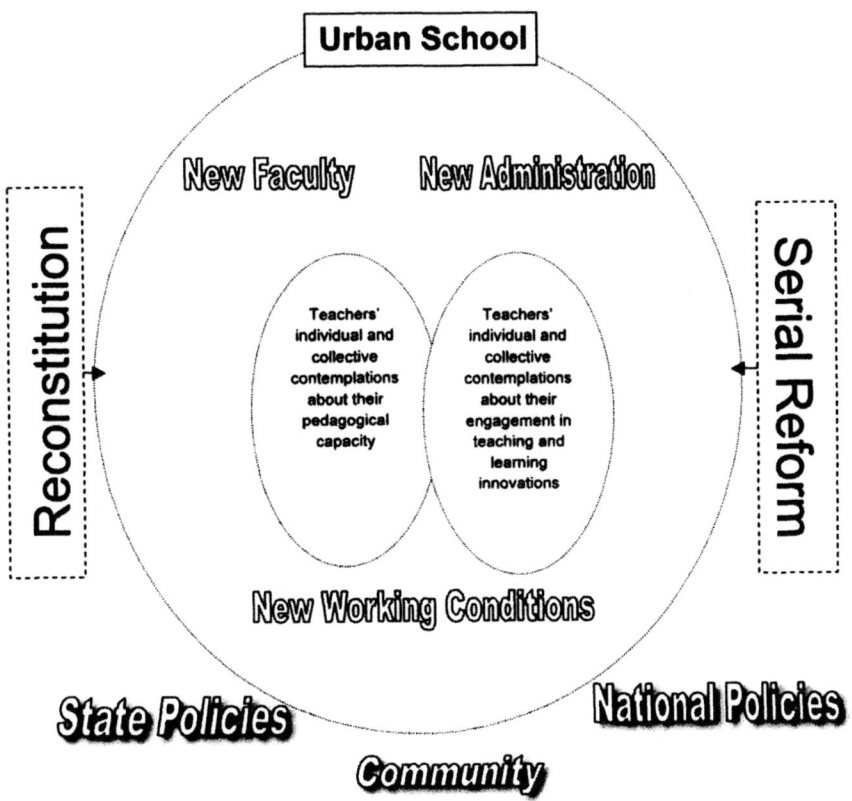

Figure A. The Context of Reform and Capacity for Teaching and Learning Innovations

The Theory of School Reform

This book takes up the intersection among teachers' historical, theoretical, political, and practical understandings about urban schools, policy driven school reform (as a source of capacity), and teaching and learning. These understandings individually have lead to an array of commentaries, studies, policies, and assumptions. Bodies of literature that not only depict issues of urban schools, policy driven school reform, and teaching and learning in particular ways but also problematize them are valuable to the broader conversation of student success and school effectiveness and improvement. Many of those theoretical and practical implications are taken up in this text and are discussed, mutually, in the context of the working lives of real teachers. Yet, here, they, along with the contemplations of a unique group of teachers, are further situated and analyzed for the purpose of understanding the nexus between teaching and learning.

For example, *A Nation at Risk* (National Commission on Excellence in Education, 1983) represents a significant marker for contemporary school reform agendas. This report ushered in a belief that the quality of U.S. public education was quickly falling behind that of foreign nations. A major concern toward maintaining the strength of the United States' global economic power ensued. The document declared that, "If an unfriendly foreign power had attempted to impose on America the mediocre educational performance that exists today, we might well have viewed it as an act of war" (p. 5). An interest in the state of affairs for school reform began to take a national focus—a focus that prompted greater national control over public school reform. This end was achieved through the means of federal policy, particularly the reauthorization of the Elementary and Secondary Educational Act.

New demands for educational change birthed various waves of reform. Each of these waves brought with it a new language to describe school change as well as new approaches toward school change. Each approach toward school change also brought with it its own theory-of-action. These theories-of-action attempt to explain, predict, or control human behavior and make certain assumptions about these behaviors as contained within the conditions in which these behaviors are to take place (Argyris & Schön, 1974). As such, each approach toward school change makes assumptions about and affects the daily lives of teachers' work.

One assumption made is that staff development (also known as professional development) is needed to improve the quality of practicing teachers. Griffin (1987) contends that, "staff development is school improvement and professional growth" (p. 33). Therefore, staff development, school reform, and school improvement all become important variables that affect the quality of teaching and learning. Thus, staff development that attempts to bring about some level of change in teachers' practices needs to be context sensitive, paying attention to the conditions that mediate teachers' work (Griffin, 1987). The assumption that staff development is needed to improve the quality of practicing teachers simultaneously suggests that, as part of the reform process of schools, teachers also need to undergo some sort of change. In this regard, staff development programming becomes a vehicle that manages and encourages changes in teachers' beliefs, knowledge, and practices and a change in the quality of the core technology of schooling.

The aim of school improvement sought through policy driven reforms that impact teaching and learning is made even more complex within the context of urban schools. Literature has built a case that describes inner-city, urban schools as places filled with racial, ethnic, and language minority students; students who come from low-income families; and students who perform poorly on standardized tests. In addition, an overwhelming majority of minority and low-income students are relegated to classrooms of poor teacher quality (Darling-Hammond, 2007; Harris & Herrington, 2006) and poor facilities (Kozol, 1991). For example, Anyon (1997), analyzing the economics of urban schooling, reports of the deteriorated conditions of Newark Public School system during the 1990's while under the threat of state takeover. After unannounced visits to 50 out of 82 schools, independent evaluators concluded, "Children in the Newark public schools . . . endure degrading school environments that virtually ensure academic failure. . . . [In many classrooms] there is nothing. . . . Science laboratories lack basic equipment" (p. 144). In addition, low-performing, low-income areas with large numbers of minority students are more likely to experience inconsistent staffing from year to year, as well as an influx of inexperienced teachers compared to their counterparts of high-performing, high-income, and predominately White schools (Johnson, Berg, & Donaldson, 2005).

The intersections of these understandings about urban schools, policy driven reform, and teaching and learning support the conceptual framework described in Figure A. in a way that connections can be made between policy driven school reforms designed to build capacity and teachers' contemplations about their pedagogical capacity to engage in teaching and learning innovations. The context of these connections consists of an inner-city, urban elementary school and its teachers' working conditions as mediated by the multiple policy driven reforms. More specifically, the central connectors of these variables are school reconstitution and the implementation of serial CSRs, each operating within its own theory-of-action. Yet, each of these variables has been studied, written about, and problematized in ways that are not always complementary; therefore, understanding the relationships between teachers' contemplations about pedagogical capacity and their engagement in teaching and learning innovations is made even more complex, more provocative, and more meaningful.

Furthermore, as an educator who has taught in suburban, inner-city, and even urban reconstituted schools, I have come to believe and understand the endeavor of schooling to be an enterprise of cultural and ideological production. As such, schooling not only supports relationships that legitimates dominant society (Giroux, 1981) and perpetuates a politics of official knowledge (Apple, 1996) resulting in the manifestation of a banking system (Friere, 1970) that functions to oppress the critical consciousness of its pupils and teachers, but also produces and (re)inscribes its structural function in ways that define the organization of districts and schools as well as their place in society as common sense. This is not to say that schools are not also site of emancipatory endeavors. These acts, however, are less of the norm and tend to require deliberate, herculean efforts on the part of their sponsors. Yet, it is the interplay among the ideological, cultural, and structural means of schooling that shapes the power relations between schools and the districts in which they exist as well as among those who work in these sites.

Collins (2009) provides a contemporary explanation of power relations as functioning systemically and in a synergistic fashion. She explains the system of power as existing within and among four domains. These are the: (1) structural, (2) disciplinary, (3) cultural, (4) and interpersonal domains. The structural domain of power operates through organizations such as schools and relegates things seemingly the way they are "without anybody doing anything" (p. 53). For example, public schools are free to all, consist of grades K-12, and are charged with preparing tomorrow's citizens and work force. The disciplinary domain of power shapes our bureaucratic and regulatory practices. In the case of schooling, students and schools are held accountable for their performance through the practice of standardized testing. The cultural domain of power justifies social and political hierarchies in ways that are often subtle and veiled. This domain is typically mediated through mass media and popular culture and works to construct our ideas and stories about schools such as the ways in which inner-city, urban schools are portrayed in movies and news reports. The interpersonal domain of power informs interpersonal relationships and behaviors, often on an individual basis. It is through this domain that contentions between public and private spaces are weighed among families and validate their school choice decisions.

These understandings are steeped in the traditions of critical theory and critical pedagogy that examine, critique, and problematize the notions of power, ideology, culture, and social relations. In order for critical theorists to better understand these notions as forces that shape and inform the practices of schooling—practices that are pedagogical—Giroux (1983) calls for a reconsideration and reformulation of "how human beings come together within specific social practices and historical contexts to make and reproduce the conditions of their existence [in schools]" (p. 120). For educators, researchers, and critical theorists, this means coming to understand those social practices that are informed by hegemonic ideologies and traditional practices—practices that define the "grammar" of schooling (Tyack & Tobin, 1994). While the dynamic forces of power and ideology may seem to work in ways that make the grammar or rules of schooling fixed, it is the critical examinations of these relations that offer up agency as a means to improve the conditions of schools and schooling.

As a researcher, my position is one that seeks to understand how the dynamics of culture, power, ideology, structure, and agency are played out in the working lives of teachers within a particular context of serial comprehensive, urban school reform. My position is to understand how these dynamics, within this context, shape teachers' understandings of their pedagogical capacity and their engagement in teaching and learning innovations in ways that are historical, theoretical, political, and practical. The dialogues with and observations of teachers working in an underperforming urban school seeking to advance student achievement help to better define the conditions that empower those with the audacity to teach.

Chapter Two
Introducing Hillside Elementary School

Hillside Elementary School, by board decree, was scheduled to become a technology-focused, reconstituted school around the time many of the tenets of the No Child Left Behind Act were being tried and tested in Texas and leading up to the presidency of G. W. Bush. The school had a history of low performance on standardized tests and struggled to undo the image painted by chronic low performance on the statewide assessment. Reconstitution was just one option the district's board of education took in order to turn the school around. Hillside is located is located in one of the district's poorest communities and hosts a 99.9% African American student population.

Politics of Finesse

Similar to other reported cases of school reconstitution in which the reform is rolled out under the pressure of a rigid time schedule (Rice & Malen, 2002), the board announced the policy enactment in January, thereby allowing seven months for full implementation. Furthermore, the board had aborted its plan to redesign the school as a technology magnet school, but wrote in a provision that would allow for continued discussions to broker the possibility of phasing in a magnet program in years to come. The hope of converting Hillside to a technology magnet school was part of the District's broader plan to recruit and retain, within the district, children of high-income families from throughout the district. Just as the San Francisco Unified School District felt the direct pressure of court order to reconstitute certain schools in order to achieve racial balance among its student populations in 1983 (Goldstein et al., 1998), the policy enactment to reconstitute Hillside Elementary also arose from similar political positions around the school's racial composition. According to both principals, the board's decree and discussions about the school's future arose from a highly race-based political position. According to Ms. Abbey, the principal during my dialogues and observations with teachers, "At the time [of the board's decree] there was a great deal of discussion in the district around revisiting desegregation." Mr. Thachery, the former principal, recalled that the plan to phase in a magnet program that would attract White families from other communities in the district was unexpectedly foiled by the school's physical appearance. He explained that, upon being transferred from within the district to become the principal of Hillside,

> The extent of what [information] I was given as a principal about what this [school] should look like or what it would involve was that it was going to be a technology school. This is what they [district officials] said: "We re-wired the building, put in another computer lab and that all the classrooms would have computers." And, that's what made it a technology institute.

However, no major changes had been made to the facade of the school in preparation for its reconstitution. According to Mr. Thachery, when middle class (mostly White) families visited the school in consideration of their children attending a technology magnet school, the physical state of the school left these parents with little desire to transfer their children. To date, Hillside Elementary has not yet become a technology magnet school. Instead, the school was reconstituted as a technology *theme* school with a 99.9% African American student population from the surrounding, low-income community.

At play within the district during this transition period was a politics of finesse. Jones and Malen (2002) drew from their research on reconstituted schools to define a politics of finesse as occurring when certain groups seek to enact policies through the savvy use of internal negotiations. Regarding the racial composition of Hillside, Ms. Abbey explained:

> Some reorganization sessions were going on and some of the discussions made me feel very uncomfortable that parents and community others—some, not all, certainly not all—were advocating that African American children should stay in their own communities and not come into other communities.

A politics of finesse directly affected the implementation process during the reconstitution of Hillside Elementary, even beyond race issues. Informal conversations with the former principal revealed that his decision to move to Hillside was limited by district constraints. In fact, several searches for a principal had taken place prior to his appointment. The first of these was a national search, followed by a local search, both of which failed to yield a board-approved candidate. Mr. Thachery, who was the principal of another elementary school within the district—a school on the rise from being a chronically, low-performing school, which had recently won a national award for its performance as a Title I school—had not applied for the job. Yet, the board chose to offer him the head administrative position for Hillside with the intent that he would turn the school around. Mr. Thachery recalled that he was surprised by the offer because he had only been a principal for a few years. He was also reluctant to take the position because of the promising changes at his then current school; however, the offer to lead Hillside was non-negotiable. Mr. Thachery explained that the board's offer was presented under conditions that seemed to infer that to decline the position would impinge his continued employment within the district as a principal. Thus, Mr. Thachery's relocation highlights the board's use of what Collins refers to as disciplinary power (2009), though veiled by savvy internal negotiations. These examples demonstrate how the implementation of school reform, particularly the reconstitution of Hillside, often emerges through a politics of race and a politics of internal negotiations that exert power and control. These conditions exemplify a politics of finesse.

Mr. Thachery's Leadership at Hillside

With little direction beyond the charge to go forth and create changes at Hillside Elementary, Mr. Thachery was left, by and large, to his own devices to create a mission for the school while focusing on the creative use of technology as a tool to raise student achievement scores. Other than to turn the school around from its status of persistently low performance, no deadline for such success was given, nor was he told what direction he should take in order to do so. In many ways, reconstitution ushered in a grassroots reform in which Mr. Thachery was given leeway to design the internal network, goals, mission, and vision of Hillside. As a first step toward bringing about change, Mr. Thachery explained:

> There were a number of discipline and other issues [at the school] too; so, the idea for me was to hire people who understood the challenges of working in a low performing, all African American, low-income school and community, and, to hire people who clearly understood the dynamics of the demands that they would have been expected to meet [based on these conditions]. One thing that I looked for were people who would be receptive to what may have been perceived to be unconventional ways of teaching in the elementary environment. I really wanted people who wanted to be there, who knew what they were getting into and who would be up for the challenge.

Consistent with reconstitution research that explains the reform's theory-of-action as being steeped in the expectation that a reconstituted school's new teacher composition will ignite new and inventive teaching practices (Malen et al., 2002), Mr. Thachery also envisioned Hillside as a school where teachers would begin to perceive urban teaching in non-traditional ways. Drawing from his experiences as a principal of another school within the district, Mr. Thachery elaborated:

> I believe very much in the value of teaming and working in an interdisciplinary fashion . . . also in developing more of a data orientation to what you would do to improve student performance, and what that would mean in terms of staff development needs for teachers.

While these approaches to collaboration are commonplace in today's school reform planning, they were quite novel and still formative during the early 2000s. In short, this principal's plan was to reconceptualize staff development as part and parcel of the teachers' daily work fiber. This meant building into teachers' weekly schedule a double planning period in which they would be able to meet routinely for two class periods as a grade level team. According to Mr. Thachery, these meetings—meetings that were still in practice during my visit to the school—were designed to build collegial relationships among teachers and to break traditional thinking about the onus of student learning as residing within a single classroom. His vision was to help teachers "start thinking that they are collectively responsible for all of the kids at a particular grade level." This type of thinking about school design and school reform supports the development of Professional Learning Communities (DuFour & Eaker,1998; DuFour, 2004) and what Darling-Hammond (2005) refers to as the essential recognition of time needed to build trust among teachers throughout the process of developing collaborative relationships—relationships that unsettle isolation and a "keep it to yourself," or "closed-door ethic" among teachers whereby "one's work stops before infringing upon the space of others" (Easley, Henning, & Bradley, 2003, p. 59). Mr. Thachery believed in the value of collegiality and a unified focus on student learning. He also held a high regard for reshaping teachers' traditional thinking about instructional planning and their private cogitations about teaching and learning. He repeatedly expressed a need to unsettle what Sergiovanni (1997) calls teachers' traditional instructional "theories-of-acceptability," that is, traditional thinking about schools that go unquestioned.

The task of unsettling traditional thinking is intensified in the context of reconstitution, for like other reconstituted schools (Malen et al., 2002), approximately 75% of Hillside's new faculty consisted of first-year teachers and many others with less than three years of teaching experience. In order to unearth their divergent theories-of-acceptability, Mr. Thachery conceptualized teachers' double planning time as an opportunity for unifying instructional support and collaborative professional development. These sessions were designed to shape teachers' thinking about teaching and learning to the extent that they would be expected to openly discuss instructional issues and student learning by beginning from a central focal point: that being an attention to student learning assessment data (primarily classroom generated data). Mr. Thachery understood the focus on students' existing levels of achievement as a means to both synchronize teachers' discussions about their teaching practices as well as to elevate said levels of achievement. Thus, the prime goal of these meetings was for teachers to collectively learn to become more effective with the population of students they served through a systematic process of goal oriented and shared decision making. Mr. Thachery explained:

> It [the double planning time] was devoted to data analysis, using data to plan lessons. It was to get feedback and allow them time to do observations in other classrooms or other schools. It was an [professional development] opportunity for me to bring in other people to work with them around instructional issues. And that proved to be very helpful. It really was a good way for me to be able

to tie the data we had to what they were doing. The teachers did all of their grade reporting electronically. They had a requirement to turn in those [student achievement data] reports every other week. I wanted to see the results of their classroom assessment, and we had an efficiency target, and I checked to see what percentage of kids were making progress on assessments. And, if kids didn't make it, they [the teachers] had to re-teach and re-test. And, I looked for that. So, the basis of that double planning period was to discuss issues like that.

Ms. Abbey's Leadership at Hillside

Ms. Abbey's relationship with Hillside Elementary began during Mr. Thachery's tenure as principal. She was initially hired by Mr. Thachery as the school's technology coordinator; yet, she later left the school for a promotion elsewhere in the district. Three years later, Ms. Abbey returned to Hillside as its principal, following Mr. Thachery's decision to accept a high-ranking position in another school district. Hillside was her first principalship. Due to a reduction in student enrollment, the vice principal's position was recently cut. For all practical purposes, Hillside represented the initial testing ground for the fledgling principal.

Ms. Abbey inherited a school in the throes of physical renovations as well as on a path of declining student enrollment, due in part to changing housing patterns among local families. Many of the original staff members were still present despite the fact that some had been displaced, in part, because of budget cuts associated with the withering student enrollment. To her delight, she found that the plans for technology expansion and renovations were under way. Ms. Abbey acknowledged that these were important factors regarding her return because she was witnessing the manifestation of many changes she helped to initiate as the technology coordinator. Yet, during the time of my visit to the school, many of those plans had been scaled back, resulting in a single lab of 20 functioning computers to be shared among the less than 300 student body. The three to five computers in each classroom were installed with district approved enrichment programs for reading and mathematics, and these were used primarily to track students' progress towards skills development. There was no on-site technology coordinator. The initial technological theme that distinguished the reconstituted school was by and large in name only.

Despite the recent upgrades and small gains on the state test, Ms. Abbey believed that many of the public's negative perceptions of the school continued to prevail. These included a low regard for the academic potential of the student population as well as a stigma of persistent failure. Ms. Abbey's dedication to the school and its students, in particular, was grounded in her ideal that "Education is the only clear path to change conditions and to make a break in the poverty cycle in order to improve life." Her conviction is consistent with the belief that, "Virtually everyone in America agrees that a good education is an essential foundation for success in terms of the material, social and civic aspects of American life" (Hirschland & Steinmo, 2003, p. 334). Ms. Abbey grew up in the same neighborhood as the children of Hillside and recalled that a committed and passionate African American teacher made a difference in her life. She explained that this teacher gave her the vision and the desire to do well in school and to achieve in life. Ms. Abbey was driven by her belief that "Too many times our kids, African American kids, are written off and are not expected to excel academically." In this respect, she agreed with the connotative tenet of the NCLB that promised to leave no child behind academically. To ensure that the administration and teachers at Hillside made good on the promise to leave no child behind, and understanding that achievement also rests in the efforts of children and their parents, Ms. Abbey explained, "We tell our students to coope-rate, work your hardest, and put your effort into school because you are only helping yourself when you do well." Yet, in order for children to excel academi-cally, Ms. Abbey insisted that students have to find value in school. She believed that the work of educators should be guided by principles that motivate students to want to attend school and want to do well academically. In her words:

> They [the children] need to know that we care about them. We also have high
> expectations for them and in this area where it's considerably depressed—
> there's a lot of gang activity, drug activity, parents are missing in action,
> grandparents are doing the rearing—they need people who believe in them and
> can, everyday, say, "Hey, it's worth coming down here to this building because
> we've got something really good for you."

A Context in Flux

Since its reconstitution, Hillside Elementary experienced various significant changes that impacted the nature of teaching and learning. Examples of these changes include a dwindling student enrollment, the adoption of comprehensive curriculum reforms, and the enactment of NCLB. Hillside Elementary is a community school that is heavily populated with children from several surrounding public housing projects. Yet, due to the gentrification of central city areas, as in Chicago and Atlanta, many of the public housing projects have been and are being slowly evacuated, demolished, and replaced with smaller, mixed-income, family developments. As a result of this slow transformation, as well as the usual migrant nature of many of the low-income families within the district, Hillside was undergoing a steady decline in student enrollment. Ms. Abbey elaborated:

> When the projects were filled to capacity, the families had lots of children. This
> is a walking neighborhood. We at one time, I understand, had as many as 600
> students in the building. When I came we were close to 390; three schools

years later, we're at 275, and families are continuing to move and are encouraged to move because they are tearing down the housing projects.

This steady decline in student enrollment translated into fewer operational dollars for the school. Fewer operational dollars translated into fewer resources for the children who remain at the school. Yet, their needs for learning supports did not take a down turn commensurate with the reduction of financial support. Cuts in schools' budgets often force teachers and administrators to rethink their work to meet the demands of raising student achievement in the context of diminishing capacity as related to a decline in resources (even when the reduction of resources is tantamount to the rate of student attrition). They are forced to make decisions that oftentimes reshape their teaching practices or instructional emphases. Ms. Abbey illustrated how resource reduction placed a strain on building level decision-making:

> In the spring when I did my budget, I was down to teachers and textbooks. That was it. We lost, in terms of staff, four positions because of cuts. And in a building of this nature where we are trying to extend technology but we also have needs around discipline and extra help in the classrooms, there are not a lot of choices to make.

Changes in Curriculum
Significant curricular changes at Hillside began during the tenure of Mr. Thachery with the adoption of Everyday Mathematics produced by the McGraw-Hill Publishing Company; a pre-packaged, inquiry-based mathematics series, which quickly translated into the school's mathematics curriculum. Also, in order to support teachers' instructional practices across content areas, Mr. Thachery redefined the role of Instructional Teacher Leaders (ITLs) as designed by the district. Understood as generalist positions assigned at the primary (grades K-2) and intermediate (grades 3-5) levels, he turned these positions into content specific appointments that resulted in the assignment of a reading ITL, a mathematics ITL, and a writing ITL. One role of these ITLs was to assist in coordinating building level professional development programs for teachers in their respective content areas.

According to Ms. Abbey, mathematics and reading had become the curricular "mantra" for Hillside. This is due, in part, to the core areas on the state assessments, students' previous performance on these assessments, and district demands to increase student achievement as measured by said assessments. While the Everyday Mathematics curriculum remained the same over the years, the school adopted the Harcourt reading program as its English language arts (reading) curriculum.[1] Ms. Abbey recalled:

> When I came we were getting ready to adopt a reading curriculum, and after consultation with a couple of people in the district and with the staff, we

decided to go ahead with the Harcourt reading curriculum. This curriculum is a

phonics approach that focuses on word decoding. This curriculum was like a goldmine, compared to what we were using, realizing that our students needed explicit and systematic curriculum that provides a type of structure for decoding and word attack.

Nevertheless, she expressed some concern regarding the resulting incongruences between the taught curriculums and students' performance outcomes on standardized assessments. More specifically, the Ms. Abbey explained: "When I'm in the classrooms and coaches [ITLs] are around and [district] people come to visit, we look like we're implementing the program the way it should be, but we are not getting the results that we expect." Ms. Abbey reported that the current curricular landscape in both reading and mathematics was being resurveyed to decide what lies at the heart of these curriculums in terms of what students must know and what parts of these curriculums have the greatest impact on student learning.

Decisions to redesign the curricular and instructional foci reflect the school's attempt to navigate between the core content of the school's curriculums and the content areas of the state assessments. More specifically, these decisions may represent the school's attempt to prioritize essential teaching and learning elements that will be rewarded (Robertson, 1996) by district and state officials based on student assessment outcomes. This means aligning central curriculum components with the demands of the statewide tests (English & Steffy, 2001).

These decisions to reconsider school curriculums can be understood as resulting from the intensification of school change and reform. Such intensification bears down on building level decision-making and teachers' work in response to the demands of district, state, and federal policies that oftentimes restrict teachers' decisions about educational change while simultaneously imposing increased measures of accountability. For Hillside Elementary School, NCLB has produced an unexpected impact as the state and district have made adjustments in order to comply with federal regulations. In a "trickle-down" effect, federal policy has rewritten the codes for which schools define their own achievement and their internal practices that aim to yield said achievement. That is, NCLB, in its attempt to improve public education, seeks to hold states and schools accountable for closing the student achievement gap by wedding performance and budget. For schools that fail to continuously produce annual yearly progress (AYP) over a two-year period and in regards to increased student achievement across disaggregated student populations, these schools run the risk of losing federal financial support. Feeling the unexpected intensification brought on by the implementation of NCLB, Ms. Abbey remarked:

Our goals though, have remained the same here at Hillside. We remain a school where children not only have exposure to state of the art technology, but that technology supports student learning at a high level. In a large sense, that's still our goal [as during the beginning of reconstitution]. However, we have another, more immediate goal, and that's with the state assessments. We are on the [state's] list for improvement, which means that we have to meet Adequate Yearly Progress this year. We now have to follow more rigid, district-driven curricular guidelines that focus on basic skills and students' universal proficiency of these skills. As a result, the technology ideas have not been set side, but the ideas around the fullest implementation of the math and reading curriculums are paramount, and, of course, anything that we can do to support that with technology, we are continuing to do.

Not only does the "trickle-down" effect of policy pose an impact on curricular decision-making at the building level, but this effect also impacts resource allotment at this level. Ms. Abbey explained some of the ways in which federal policy has had an unexpected strain on building level resources:

It hasn't turned out to be additional resources for us [as related to NCLB resource allotment for Hillside Elementary School]. The faculty has taken on the mission to leave no child behind. It's just that when I'm saying we need all children proficient, teachers are looking at me saying, "OK, we have the curriculum; we are here every day, but we need some assistance in terms of having smaller class size, in term of having after school programs that are of quality and that really connect with our work and other programs." We're just getting small measures of that. We have, for example, a [Reading First] grant through the state and federal government that targets K-3 children.[2] My concern is for the fifth grade students who take the state assessment. There is no additional assistance for fifth graders.[3]

Discussion

From these examples, it becomes clear that the context of Hillside Elementary reflects a cornucopia of change. Like most contemporary schools defined as low performing, particularly those inner-city, urban schools serving large numbers of students placed at-risk, incessant change and reform have come to define their contexts. Hillside has undergone reconstitution, a leadership change, a comprehensive change in its reading curriculum, and has had to cope with the growing demands of NCLB as well as. While reconstitution may represent the opportunity for a grassroots type reform in which Mr. Thachery hand-selected teachers and orchestrated the school's overall instructional focus, NCLB superimposed a more centralized and standardized instructional control directed by the district in a top-down fashion. In many ways, particularly in the conversations with teachers, to be discussed later, and with Ms. Abbey, NCLB has not only reoriented their understandings of reconstitution but has co-opted many of the instructional support structures introduced by Mr. Thachery during the initial stages of reform.

As illustrated in the accounts by Mr. Thachery and Ms. Abbey, top-down policy changes often alter the design, management, curricular, and instructional decision-making processes of schools. Conversely, the relationships between schools and their larger educational contexts (i.e., district, state, and federal) that exemplify the exertion of structural and disciplinary power structures remain intact. For example, districts, states, and even the federal government, under the direction of the NCLB, judge the quality of schools and their teachers by targets developed beyond the building level. Moreover, externally imposed budget and performance accountability measures (e.g., the allotment of financial resources based on students' scores on standardized tests) that simultaneously act as policy compliance incentives, may impair building level decision-making. These relationships represent a tension between externally imposed policies and a school's capacity for self-governance. This tension characterizes the context of schooling for many inner-city, urban schools like Hillside. This context, in turn, influences the quality of teaching and learning—quality as shaped by the capacity for teachers' engagement in teaching and learning innovations. Yet, because of serial reforms occurring since reconstitution, Hillside teachers' capacity has been further tested and their contextualized understandings of their capacity are both historical (marked by initial reconstitution and Mr. Thachery's principalship) and contemporary (marked by Ms. Abbey's principalship). Their understandings about contextualized capacity and engagement in teaching and learning innovations are also individual as well as collective. These understandings are to be revealed, discussed, and problematized throughout the following chapters.

Notes

1. The Everyday Mathematic of The University of Chicago School of Mathematics Project (McGraw-Hill Publishing Company) had been adopted and implemented as Hillside's mathematics curriculum. Trophies (Grade K) and Collections (Grades 1-5), both part of the Harcourt reading/language arts program, were adopted as the school's reading curriculum. Teachers tend to refer to both series by the incorporated name, Harcourt. For this reason, both are referred to in this study as the Harcourt reading curriculum/series.

2. A benefit of NCLB comes in the way of Reading First (a federal reading intervention grant program). The district has received a six-year appropriation of $16.2 million, the largest such grant the district has ever received. Hillside is one of 30 Title I schools in the district allotted Reading First money due to its low test scores and large low-income student population. This means that the school is able to fund a full-time literacy coach (Reading ITL) as well as secure specialized reading diagnostic tests for primary level students.

3. Student assessment scores on the statewide test measure whether or not a school has met Adequate Yearly Progress. This is currently determined by fifth grade scores on the state assessment.

Chapter Three
Teachers Defining Teaching and Learning Innovations

Teachers' understandings about their pedagogical capacity and their engagement in teaching and learning innovations are made complex and rich by the context of schooling, particularly in the context of a serial reform/ed/ing urban school influenced by continuous policy directives at the district and federal levels, diminishing resources, and a history of low student performance on standardized tests. Within the context of schools and schooling, teachers' work, like that of students', functions at two levels: individually and collectively. Such levels form the basis of organizational dynamics as discussed by organizational theorists like Senge (1990) and Wegner (1998). This chapter seeks to set a foundation for teachers' contextualized, individual (idiographic) and collective (nomothetic) understandings about pedagogical capacity and teaching and learning innovations, and to explore the relationships between pedagogical capacity and engagement in teaching and learning innovations as defined by teachers.

Eight teachers and two administrators engaged in a series of dialogues with me as a researcher and opened their classrooms, offices, and meetings for frequent observations. In addition, four other teachers served in a supporting role by participating in a single dialogue with me. Of the eight teachers, all were women (five White and three African American). This racial composition directly reflects the school's 63% White and 37% African American faculty, of which 12% were males. Each of these teachers had worked at Hillside for at least five years and had experienced a multitude of changes in the school's context—changes in curriculums and administrative and staff compositions, to name a few. What follows is a discussion of these teachers' contextualized contemplations of (1) their pedagogical capacity and (2) their engagement in teaching and learning innovations. Our initial dialogues functioned to explore teachers' nomothetic definition of teaching and learning innovations and their espoused relationship between this construct and that of pedagogical capacity.

Teaching and Learning Innovations
In a common sense manner, the notion of innovative teaching connotes an element of teacher quality. While teacher quality, at least at the federal level, has come to be understood in quantifiable measures of professionalism by counting teachers' certifications and college degrees, dialogues with teachers revealed that they have their own language and descriptors for the notion of teacher quality, particularly as related to teaching and learning innovations. When asked, "How would you describe your teaching as innovative," these Hillside teachers collectively described actions taken to differentiate their teaching.

Congruent with Miles' (1964) definition of innovation as a deliberate and intentional act used for (a) particular purpose(s), with anticipated consequences, teachers explained that instructional differentiation and calibrations are necessary to meet the varied needs of the students in their classrooms. A majority of them added that this is achieved in creative and/or "inventive" ways. While their descriptions were diverse, the beliefs about what makes their teaching innovative were consistent. Teachers unanimously defined teaching and learning innovations as the differentiated/calibrated instructional and classroom practices that address the individual and diverse learning needs of students (e.g. learning styles, functional levels, motivation, etc.). For example, teachers explained:

> My teaching is extremely innovative because I deal with so many students learning at different levels. . . . I have to teach the same thing to each one of them, but all at a different level. (Ms. Jefferson)

And,

> I try hard to address all the different areas of teaching, all the different needs of the children, the auditory, the visual. And I know that I am innovative in the fact that I come up with new techniques [to meet these different needs/modalities]. (Ms. Adele)

These examples represent teachers' thoughts about differentiated instructional practices that address the diverse learning needs of multiple students. However, teaching and learning innovations (TLIs) also include calibrated practices that address a collective need of students. Ms. Smith, a veteran teacher of 13 years, described how being innovative requires a great deal of creativity to meet the learning needs of students. She equated innovation with creativity and explained how she calibrated her teaching/classroom practices to meet the learning needs of multiple students who shared the same need to associate orthographic symbols of letters with their corresponding phonemic/phonetic systems:

> I'd say that for me being creative is trying to take from the curriculum and building from that, trying to do something different. For instance, I was trying to get the students to learn letters and sounds, and I was having a hard time doing that. So, in the phonics lesson, I taught them a song according to the tune "Who Let The Dogs Out." [singing] 'Who let the "A" out [singing the short letter sound] a, a, a, a? Who let the "B" out b, b, b, b?' I thought that was very innovative. To me that's creative, trying to think of something that's going to gain their attention, to motivate them, to energize them. That [song] did it. They are now remembering those letters, remembering those sounds. They can make the connections through that tune. Those are the things I have to do— using the curriculum but yet adapting it so that the students can understand it a

little bit better, [adapting it] to their own lives, [adapting it] to their own experiences.

From these examples (and others to follow), it is easy to see that the teachers of Hillside believed that differentiating/calibrating their practices in creative and inventive ways is necessary in order to support students' learning and, in some cases, to jump start students' learning. As demonstrated by Ms. Smith, these aims are also achieved by calibrating her traditional practices—as existing within and defined by the confines of Hillside's text book driven curriculums—for the purpose of making the curriculums conceptually obtainable and meaningful, and to make the curriculums come to life. Her aim is met by using media and popular culture as a source for motivating students and connecting classroom skills to the outside world that is familiar to the children she teaches. Literature on teacher quality links such innovations to cultural relevant instruction and teacher efficacy. Research reveals that effective teaching is a complex task that employs a range of teaching styles (Darling-Hammond, 2000; Clark & Peterson, 1986). This research also reveals that effective teachers readily adjust their styles to meet the needs of students. Darling-Hammond (2000) asserts that, in research on effective teaching, there is no single, silver bullet, instructional strategy that meets the diverse learning needs of students. She contends that effective teachers skillfully use a broad range of approaches such as direct instruction, modifying the use of wait time, and conceptual and experience-based learning.

Moving between instructional strategies to meet the diverse learning needs of students is just one example of TLIs. Effective teachers also calibrate/differentiate non-instructional practices in support of student learning. These too are TLIs. These innovations account for teachers' assessments of the broader social and emotional domains that support cognitive and academic development. Yet, in order to employ these innovations, effective teachers purposefully make connections between the curriculums, the learning needs of their students, and the impact their instructional and classroom practices have on students' learning.

Teacher Commitment

For the teachers of Hillside, their willingness to tailor teaching according to students' needs speaks directly to their commitment to the particular student population they serve, and their commitment serves as one level of pedagogical capacity for their engagement in TLIs. Firestone and Pennell (1993) contend that while teachers' objects of commitment may vary considerably, "committed individuals should be internally motivated" (p. 491). Various Hillside teachers explained how their commitment emerged from within:

I knew that I wanted to work with African American children, and, in particular, African American children who are described as high risk. During my college years, I decided to become a teacher because I had part time jobs working with children, and I discovered that I loved it. My undergraduate degree was in business. I worked in the industry for three or four years, and I hated it. But, I always went back to the part time jobs working with young people, elementary-age children, and I also worked with this age group in my church. That all played a part in my becoming a teacher. (Ms. Campbell)

I didn't come into teaching until after I had been a stay-at-home mother for a while. So later in my life I came into teaching, and this is the kind of place where I wanted to teach, with this student population. (Ms. Adele)

Teachers' commitment to children can be understood, in part, by the number of years each key-participant had remained at Hillside Elementary. All of the participating teachers had taught at this school for at least five years. In fact, Ms. Adele taught at Hillside two years prior to reconstitution and reapplied for her position. She explained, "I loved it here. The kids. The atmosphere. The fact that is was going to be a technology-based school really interested me as well. And, I loved the fact that if I stayed, I would teach the same [primary] grade level."

Attracting and securing a committed teaching faculty is just one theory-of-action guiding school reconstitution (Malen et al., 2002). For the teachers in this book (75% of whom were hired by Mr. Thachery at the beginning of reconstitution), commitment appeared strong. Their commitment challenges the argument that the majority of African American students receive instruction from teachers who lack the motivation and/or the enthusiasm to effectively engage students in the learning process (Kozol, 1991; Cooper & Jordan, 2003). Commitment for many teachers at Hillside evolved from an intrinsic, ethical, and moral desire to make a difference in the lives of the students they teach. Their moral commitment is consistent with the belief shared by many urban teachers (Easley, 2006) and has been captured elsewhere in books like *To Become A Teacher: Making A Difference in Children's Lives* (Ayers, 1995). When asked why he deliberately chose to teach at Hillside versus another school with a different type of student population, Mr. Parr explained:

Each day as I go home, I feel as though I have accomplished something. I feel as though I am making a difference in the lives of children, and I feel like I'm working toward a better society because these children are the future of our society. Making these accomplishments [enhancing student learning and lives] here makes me feel a little bit more alive.

Firestone and Pennell (1993) posit that, "A commitment to students may contribute to [teachers promoting] a warm, supportive [classroom] climate" (p. 491). For these Hillside teachers, commitment to students (and their needs) fostered an environment for nurturant relationships. Lakoff (2002) defines nurturant relationships through a juxtaposition of the dichotomous moral actions informed by liberal and conservative political thought. As relevant to the teachers of Hillside, he describes nuturant relationships as deriving from liberal moral actions, which are actualized through empathetic behaviors that promote fairness, a reverence for helping those who cannot help themselves, and a high regard for protecting those who cannot protect themselves. As such, self is sustained as a means to support the well-being of others and the collective.

In schools, nurturant relationships evolve from teachers' understandings about how their work influences the lives of others, namely the children in their classrooms. Thus, as teachers ponder ways in which to engage in TLIs, ethical and moral purposes simultaneously become an issue (Adelman, 1989). Related research (Easley, 2006) on urban teachers' reasoning for entering the profession reveals a high moral regard for wanting to make a difference in either/or/both society and the lives of children. This reasoning suggests that teachers deliberately consider the impact their actions have on the lives of students. Fullan (2001) contends: "moral purpose is about both ends and means. In education, an important end is to make a difference in the lives of students. But the means of getting to that end are also crucial" (p. 13).

The teachers of Hillside also acknowledged students' broader social and emotional needs as directly affecting their learning. Thus, a commitment to children and the ethical and moral purposes that guide one's interactions with children are part and parcel of the crucial means (the pedagogical capacity) for making a difference in students' lives. Ms. Appleyard explained how the social and emotional needs of students are recognized and addressed in her class:

> Some of the students in my classroom come to school from difficult family situations, and we all know that personal situations [that are social and/or emotional] always factor into things that you are doing. But these kids are little kids who are still learning to deal with and resolve problems that happen outside of school and may not have anything to do with here, but "How do I deal with it? I am a child." I know that if something bad happens to me outside of work, I know how to keep myself going. That's a life lesson that these kids are still struggling to learn. It is today's life, today's society. . . . It is my job to help these kids realize that any situation can be turned into a positive situation.

By addressing students' social and emotional concerns, teachers' nurturant relationships implicate an ethical/moral practice. They recognize these relationships as a means that supports their engagement in TLIs. Nurturant relationships between teachers and students not only provide the pedagogical capacity for teachers' engagement in TLIs, but also axiomatically place students' learning needs at the center of such innovations.

Nurturant Relationships

Reflecting upon research on the contextualized workplace relationships between students and teachers, McLaughlin (1993)[1] explains that, "Students were the basic referents as teachers talked about their schools, colleagues, classrooms, and commitment to teaching" (p. 81). This finding is particularly significant when compared to the workplace context of Hillside's teachers. McLaughlin's report reveals that:

> Teachers' comments about the aspects of their students that had the greatest impact on their classroom practices focused on the cultural diversity of students in their classrooms and on the demands, difficulties and [socioeconomic] pressures associated with today's [culturally diverse] students [such as family dysfunctions and lack of support from the family and/or the larger community]. (p. 82)

Like those in the McLaughlin study, the teachers of Hillside also worked with students who faced similar pressures. As well, the majority the teachers worked with students whose racial, ethnic, and cultural backgrounds were different from their own. The teachers at Hillside readily talked about their relationships with students in ways that recognized the despair in their students' home lives. Yet, unlike many of the secondary teachers in the McLaughlin study, the Hillside teachers spoke candidly about supporting the academic growth of students by offsetting some of the perceived ills of the children's home environments. In this regard, the classroom represents a caring, safe and "warm" place. Such classrooms are testaments of nurturant relationships that attend to the emotionality of learning. Several teachers described their nurturant relationships with students:

> My philosophy as a teacher is a lot like that of a mother. I set my goals very high for my students, but not so high that they can't obtain them. I know that the goals I have for them are all obtainable by each one of them, though at different levels. But I do expect the best out of them. (Ms. Jefferson)

She continued:

> I talk to my students a lot. We talk about their tests, their grades, how they feel, school, and things at home if they want to talk about that. We talk about these things because I think it is important that I build a relationship with them. Then if something is bothering them, they are able to come to me and we can talk about it. They know that I'm here [for support].

> I think my classroom is a pleasant place, a comfortable setting. That's what I try to provide for the children—a comfortable, relaxed, low stress, environment. They have enough stress at home. (Ms. Day)

Ms. Lenora summarized:

> Especially since they are coming with so many different things at home or whatever might be affecting them, I have had kids who were low performers in the morning. Sometimes this is because they come to school hungry and/or they just weren't interested in what's going on. Getting to know each and individual kid, and trying to understand what motivates them and what they have going on, and understanding these things, lets me know how to deal with each child. But, I can't deal with all them in the same way.

While each of these voices registers compassion for students' academic achievement, each captures teachers' deep commitment for students as a human endeavor. This level of commitment embraces students' need for support—support that not only recognizes students as individuals, each with his/her own specialized learning needs, but support for their basic social and emotional needs as well. These voices explain the importance of calibrating ones classroom practices (e.g., building nurturant relationships with individual and collective students as a TLI).

These voices also convey an important, yet generally unspoken constitution that fuels nurturant relationships between students and their committed teachers. This is a constitution of care and trust. Trust between students and teachers, however, does not occur spontaneously. Teachers have to care for and respect students in order to seek students' trust. In turn, students have to recognize teachers' care and respect in order to extend their own trust to teachers. Some educational theorists propose that care is established through a relationship between the "carer" and the recipient (Noddings, 1992; Danielewicz, 2001); Danielewicz further explains that "Caring relations 'cannot be achieved by formula' but follow unique paths forged by individuals involved in the encounter in response to each other and the social setting" (p. 165). The same holds true for trust. For these teachers, care is inextricable from—yet helps to form—trusting relationships with students. A constitution of care and trust, however, takes time to develop as relationships between teachers and students are formed within a social context. This constitution comes to define nurturant relationships.

In an effort to demonstrate that they care for children and in an effort to build the trust necessary for nurturant relationships, teachers often have to make ethical/moral decisions about their use of time. For example, Ms. Campbell (a fifth grade teacher) explained one way in which she fosters nurturant relationships by describing how she often deals with students' social frustrations:

> I try to get a handle on things [the social problems among students] before they become too big. For example, kids might have problems with other students. I make sure that I let them know that they should come and tell me what the problem is so that we can talk about it and get it settled before it turns into a fight. Some of the girls have come to me with "He said, she said," which may

seem petty to other people, but to them, that's a real thing and that's important.
So, I listen to them and bring all the parties together, and I listen to all sides [of
the story]. By doing this and by letting them know that they can talk to me
helps [keep] things from escalating.

Through informal observations, I often witnessed Ms. Campbell talking
with individual students after class, during times that are generally scheduled as
her individual planning time. At first glance, one might assume that these
sessions are for the sole purpose of maintaining classroom order by "handling"
students' social problems before they became worse; however, these sessions of
counsel represent much more.

Ms. Campbell's talks with students represent a particular view of time. In
this context time is recognized as an essential part of the process for building
trust—an element of nurturant relationships. These talks convey to students that
their well-being is important and that their teacher cares enough to invest her
own time to support their well-being. Simultaneously, these talks represent a
common conflict between teachers and educational leaders (at the federal, state,
district and even building levels), for time has long been a predominant barrier
to school change. This is particularly true for schools undergoing drastic reform
efforts to improve student achievement (like reconstitution). Hargreaves (1994)
explains that school administrators and teachers have often conceptualized time
incongruently, particularly the demands placed on teachers' time. As such,
teachers often find themselves in a race against externally imposed time
constraints. These constraints often reflect the force of disciplinary power that
dictates how teachers should spend and account for each minute of the instructional day. Reforms that dictate to teachers how to use their time simultaneously
impose bureaucratic control over teaching. Rowan (1995) describes these
reforms as employing mechanistic strategies of practice. For example, school
districts may implement behavior controls such as increased teacher evaluation
and/or student testing, which operate as an output control to determine the rate
of teachers' instructional effectiveness. Within said reforms, teachers' time is
regarded as a commodity that can be controlled by instructional demands (e.g.,
direct instruction, teaching to the text, and attending district approved workshops on effective teaching). These reform models tend to disregard teachers'
time as existing outside of a fixed instructional template. Yet, in order for teachers to develop relationships with students, time needs to be conceptualized as a
resource that accompanies teachers' ethical/moral attention to students. This
level of attention recognizes and is responsive to the unexpected (social,
emotional, and academic) needs of students. The reconceptualization of time,
within this perspective, honors the movements, interactions, and struggles that
teachers and students engage in together throughout the academic process. In
fact, nurturant relationships that support TLIs do not take time away from
instructional demands in a destructive manner. Time, in this regard, is managed

from a teacher's ethical/moral reasoning to enhance the learning process for students.

Discussion

For the teachers of Hillside, their definition of innovative teaching is contextualized by the social, emotional, as well as the academic needs of their students. Their commitment to the students reflects a level of intrinsic pedagogical capacity. Teachers' commitment to students also shapes their ethical/moral reasoning regarding nurturant relationships, as mediated through trust and care. In turn, as teachers learn more about the social, emotional, and academic needs of students through nurturant relationships, their commitment to students is strengthened. Hence, correlations between teachers' commitment to students and their nurturant relationships characterize a level of contextualized pedagogical capacity for engagement in TLIs (See Figure B.). However, research shows that "teachers' sense of efficacy is not a global trait" (McLaughlin, 1993, p. 81) and that their attempts to rethink and align their teaching practices around the needs of students are not only idiographic, but are also contextually variant. These variants include (but are not exclusive to) the racial and socioeconomic status (SES) of students (Metz, 1993), the cultural diversity of students (McLaughlin, 1993), and the content areas taught by teachers (Darling-Hammond, 2000). For example, Ms. Lenora explained that as she learns the conditions affecting individual students' motivational needs, her interactions with students are calibrated accordingly.

What surfaces is an awareness that teaching and learning is contextualized by relationships between students and teachers. As revealed through dialogues with teachers at Hillside, these relationships are defined by the academic, social, and emotional needs of students and teachers' ethical/moral decisions to calibrate their work around these needs. Yet, the relationships between students and teachers are mediated through conditions that define the formal process of schooling as well as those conditions that shape students' needs. When the social, emotional, and academic needs of students impose upon the prescriptive processes of schooling, schooling is made dynamic. When teachers' ethical /moral decisions to build nuturant relationships with students challenge the prescriptive processes of schooling, such as teachers' use of time, understanding teachers' contextualized pedagogical capacity to engage in TLIs is made invaluable. Teachers' pedagogical capacity, as a subversive act, may be of particular importance to students of school reform and advocates for student learning.

This chapter reveals that at the center of teachers' contemplations about pedagogical capacity and their engagement in TLIs lies a concern for students' needs. In response to these needs, pedagogical capacity for engagement in TLIs is garnered through and is qualified by teachers' commitment to and their nurturant relationships with students. In essence, the dynamics of a commitment to address the holistic needs of students through nuturant relationship act as a critical link between teachers' pedagogical capacity and their engagement in TLIs. The following chapters further develop teachers' individual and collective understandings of the relationships between their pedagogical capacity and engagement in TLIs. The subsequent chapters explore broader concerns regarding students' needs, teachers' interpretations of these needs, teachers' instructional calibrations in response to these interpretations, as well as the ways in which these (and other factors) are contextually mediated through conditions in and around Hillside Elementary School.

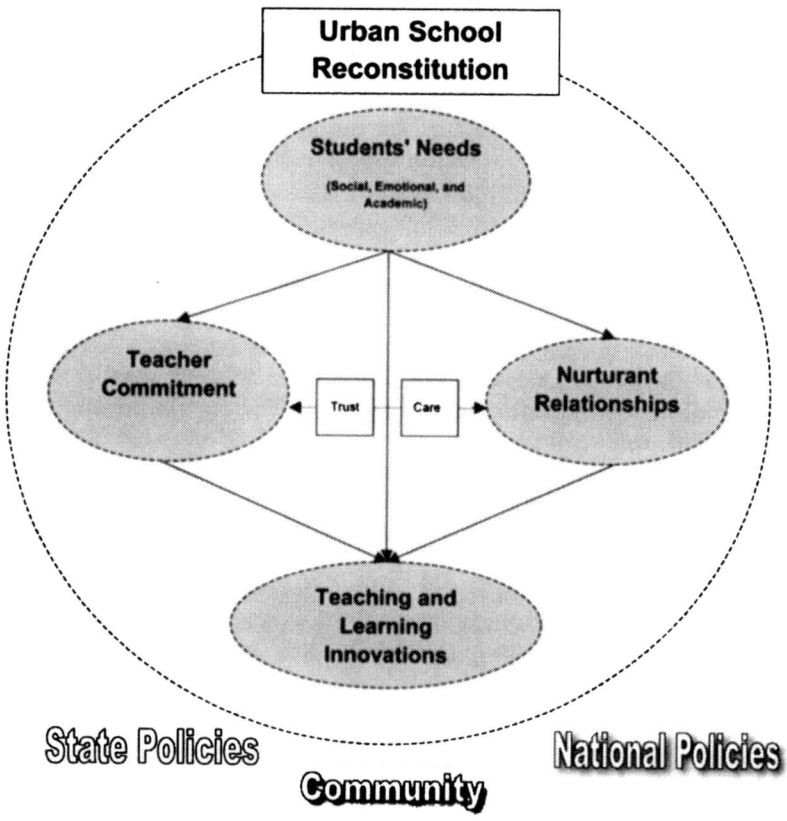

Figure B. Pedagogical Capacity that Defines Contextualized Teaching and Learning Innovations

Notes

1. This research was conducted for the Center for Research on the Context of Secondary School Teaching (CRC) at Stanford University with funding from the U.S. Department of Education Office of Research and Improvement. This three-year research project involved fieldwork and surveys in 16 public and private secondary schools located n eight different communities in two U.S. states.

Chapter Four
Critical Correspondences of Pedagogical Capacity

Rosenholtz (1991) asserts that because teachers in different schools work within different conditions, they understand schools differently. Teachers who work with different groups of students whose needs vary may come to understand teaching differently as well. Following this logic, teachers' contemplations about their pedagogical capacity to engage in teaching and learning innovations (TLIs) are likely to differ from classroom to classroom, even within the context of a single learning institution like Hillside Elementary School. These divergent perceptions may reveal contradictions. For example, all of the teachers I dialogued with explicitly expressed a commitment to the school's particular student population. Yet, Firestone and Pennell (1993) explain that commitment to students may result in a supportive climate "but may not contribute much to [their] academic achievement, while a commitment to teaching [and students' learning] may have the opposite effect" (p. 491). Herein lies a critical correspondence (Robertson, 1996) in that the teachers at Hillside expressed a commitment to students; yet, the school continued to remain low achieving on standardized assessments. Ms. Abbey, the principal explained that, "when I'm in the classrooms and coaches [ITLs] are around and [district] people come to visit, we look like we're implementing the program the way it should be, but we are not getting the results that we expect." This is just one occurrence of a critical correspondence within the reforming Hillside. Robertson (1996) explains critical correspondence as the dynamic of contradictions within reforms and that the possibility for social change is made possible when such contradictions are made explicit. Thus, making explicit and engaging such critical correspondences may very well provide the opportunities of institutional improvements for student success.

School reform is usually initiated vertically, from the top down, and from the outside inward, as is the case for school reconstitution in which schools are acted upon by policy juggernauts. Elmore (1979) observes that this vertical process traditionally begins at the top, delineates the processes of implementation, and identifies measurable outcomes. He refers to this process as forward mapping. This process is thought to provide schools with the capacity to actualize particular outcomes identified within the process. While forward mapping may delineate particular expectations for implementation and outcomes, policy often is constructed beyond the consideration of local school contexts. Yet, context directly shapes the ways in which individuals interpret policy and respond to its regulations. For classroom teachers, policy implementation generally refers to curricular and teaching demands. Outcomes are usually measured by student achievement on standardized assessments. This chapter explores the critical correspondences of the top-down, forward mapping process of policy enactment and implementation—a process that may often disregard the complex contexts of local schools. By doing so, this chapter simultaneously explores the meanings and functions of top-down curricular and assessment mandates as interpreted by teachers of Hillside Elementary School. Finally, this chapter seeks to make explicit how these mandates affect teachers' idiographic and nomothetic contemplations about their pedagogical capacity to engage in TLIs.

While the many of the perspectives reflect teachers' collective analyses, in some instances the voices of certain teachers are presented more frequently because of the clarity of their comments. Their frequent comments, except when identified as an individual or unique perspective, represent the shared perceptions of their colleagues.

Critical Correspondence of Assessment

Ms. Abbey reported that Hillside Elementary School failed to meet AYP as measured by student outcomes on the state assessment. Along with 30 other schools in the district that also failed to meet AYP, Hillside was experiencing what she called "district-driven curricular guidelines that focus on basic skills and students' universal proficiency of these skills." These guidelines include mandatory assessments that were administered at the beginning of the school year. These assessments are diagnostic instruments used to identify students' particular skills deficiencies in reading and mathematics. Regarding the reading diagnostic instrument, Ms. Brown, Hillside's Literacy Coach (Reading ITL), explained that "[the district] want[s] these tests so that all children in every school in our district are measured by the same tool." In other words, the district mandate for a standardized diagnostic assessment supports curricular alignment across schools, particularly for low-performing schools participating in the national Reading First Program for grades K-3. As teachers began to discuss assessment issues, a dichotomy arose between formal and informal assessments. From her perspective, Ms. Brown made clear that the district expects teachers to use formal reading diagnostic results as a beginning point for instructional planning, but added that not all teachers seem to follow this plan. She explained that some teachers might not clearly understand this purpose of the reading diagnostic assessments, in particular. Ms. Brown speculated that, "Many teachers may see them as just an additional test." Herein lies Ms. Brown's view of an incongruence between the value the district and its teachers' place on standardized assessments.

Teachers, however, expressed a different perspective of formal (standardized) and informal assessment practices. Beginning with formal assessment, Ms. Day, who spoke from a nurturant position, noticed that students (at the primary level) seem not to like school as they did in years prior. She explained that because of the new demands for the school to make AYP, the workday has intensified for both teachers and students:

> I think because the [achievement] target that the school has been put on, demands have trickled down from the state, to the district and to the school. I think it puts a lot of pressure on us as teachers, but it also puts a lot of pressure on the children because they don't have any down time, per se, and I guess I'm thinking too when I was in this grade. I didn't have to do all this stuff. The pressure is unbelievable preparing for standardized tests.

She continued to express concern for her students' well-being in relation to standardized assessments: "We started out the year with the students having to do two major assessments when they walked through the door. Is that the way you want to start the year off? I don't agree with that."

Ms. Adele expressed concern over standardized assessments through a critique of federal education policy (NCLB). She contended that the federal demands to leave no child behind were adversely affecting children's self-esteem. She explained at length:

> I had an educational psychology class when I was in college, and the professor was great. I remember him saying to us, your job as a teacher is to think of a child's brain as a beaker. Fill that beaker as full as you can get it. That's your job. But, sometimes the beaker is only so big. We are not all nuclear scientists. We are not all nuclear physicists. Some of us do the service work, but that's what makes the world go around. You cannot have all the children on the same level because they are individuals. If they have achieved everything that they can possibly do, I think we make them feel bad because they haven't done more. And I think it is very depressing for children. Instead of celebrating their achievements, all we are doing [through standardized assessments] is looking at what they can't do. That really bothers me. You want to get the beaker full, but not all of us have the same things in our heads. If we did, we would all look the same, we would all act the same, have the same ideas, but we are not all the same. And you can't expect students to be measured on the exact same scale.

Ms. Adele's position may stem from her current classroom context as the special education inclusion teacher for her grade level. She continued:

> My special education children are measured by the same standard as the child who is not special education. You cannot expect them to do the same as a child who does not have the problems that they have. I have students who are already identified at a very young age as mentally retarded. Am I going to make that boy feel bad because he can't write that complete sentence or he can't do what everyone says he has to do [on a standardized assessment].

Though in different grades, both Ms. Day and Ms. Adele are both primary level teachers. While Ms. Adele's concerns may appear more related to standards than assessment, her comments reflect an unease with the process in which standards for equal achievement gains among students are made real—through administering standardized tests that reinforce standards—and the ways in which students are emotionally affected by the public results of these tests. She clarified, "It just bothers me that in all this testing, this [students' emotional well-being] is not taken into account. The children are achieving as much as they possibly can, yet are still made to feel as though they are lacking [in ability] when they are not."

Both of these teachers articulated their concern for the emotional needs of children and highlighted their nurturant positions to support children throughout the learning process. Their concerns unearth a critical correspondence that questions the purpose of standardized assessments as a benefit for students. While a commonsense understanding of these tests suggests that standardized assessments may be used as a tool to guide instructional planning for the enhancement of students' academic growth, a minority group of teachers challenges the effects of these tests. Ms. Day and Ms. Adele, for example, questioned the extent to which these tests influence students' emotional well-being, particularly for their lower performing and special education students.

Even though the district may have placed unwavering value in standardized assessments, a majority of teachers expressed an interest elsewhere—a critical correspondence of formal assessments as a capacity builder for teachers' engagement in TLIs. They freely talked about the importance of informal and classroom-based assessments as contextualized tools to guide the calibration of their instruction. For example, Ms. Jefferson reported that she does use the results of the diagnostic test given at the beginning of the year to plan for heterogeneous ability grouping in language arts. With her, classroom assessment, however, played a greater role in her daily instructional planning. Unlike standardized assessments, classroom assessments were reported as providing the capacity for teachers to frequently modify their instructional practices. Hence, classroom and informal assessments were more likely than standardized assessments to provide a certain level of capacity for engagement in TLIs. This is a critical correspondence of formal assessment. For example, Ms. Jefferson explained that the diagnostic and standardized assessments do not show "movement" or learning gains among the students as the academic year progresses. While state and district stakeholders conceptualize formal assessment an instrument to determine the success of reform and to measure AYP, Ms. Jefferson continued:

> [through classroom assessments,] I can see that the children have progressed, even if it is by one or two percent, which may seem small to the state and others who collect the data, but that is huge for many of our kids. So, [because of the significance these small gains for some children] that means more to me than the 10 percent the state would ask for.

From this example and others to follow, classroom assessments measure continuous growth throughout the year and more directly shaped teachers' daily instructional planning.

In order to frequently check the pulse of students' growing knowledge base throughout the instructional planning and implementation process, Ms. Adele often informally asked students questions. More specifically, she advised that, "when you start into a lesson and start asking questions, and once you realize that the students have no idea [about what you are asking of them], that's when you have to back off and find more resources." Ms. Williams, who taught across grade levels, concurred:

> I look to see what they already know and what I can add to that. I take surveys and ask questions. I go about planning lesson for the children by finding out what they already know by asking them before planning a lesson. Just by questioning and answering helps.

Ms. Campbell talked about her experiences teaching mathematics at the intermediate level: "If there is a concept that I see the students really did not get, and I've taught it according to how the book says I should do, that's when I start thinking up other activities that will help them." She explained that her discovery of students' comprehension occurs through careful attention to their physical and extralinguistic expressions during a lesson, expressions such as blank stares. These examples demonstrate how informal assessment practices require teachers to remain keenly aware of students' immediate understandings.

Ms. Campbell also reported on the manner in which informal and classroom-based assessments may be used together as a check-and-balance to gauge student learning. She elaborated:

> There are other times when I thought the students understood a lesson based on their oral responses during class. They take a quiz, and I see that everybody bombed. That's when I begin to reflect on some of the other things that I can do with the lesson. We go back to that concept. I try not to move on until I at least see a light bulb.

Unveiled through dialogues with teachers is their esteem for the immediacy of informal and classroom-based assessments. These assessments are contextual, which allows teachers to make judgments about the discreet needs of students, collectively and individually. For Ms. Jefferson, these assessments report the results needed for her to value her student's continuous academic growth, regardless of how small these gains may be perceived by outside forces, and regardless of the fact that while she witnesses gains in student achievement, collectively these gains are quantifiably too small to meet Annual Yearly Progress. Classroom-based assessments seem to provide the pedagogical capacity for teachers to immediately engage in TLIs during a lesson sequence. They also tend to impact innovative teaching by providing teachers the capacity of autonomous decision-making (a form of teacher professionalism). As such, teachers are able to utilize informed instructional discretion within their own classrooms. This discretion represents the artistry of teaching in which teachers make immediate adjustments in their practices as derived from the myriad instructional decisions that occur almost simultaneously. More specifically, Rait (1995) posits that, "teachers make about 200 pedagogical decisions per class. Each decision may shift the focus of the class and its activities; hence active implementation is accompanied by continuous cycles of planning and evaluation" (p. 93).

For example, in a primary level classroom and just before grouping students for an enrichment reading lesson, Ms. Hooks used observational data gathered from a whole group activity to rethink the grouping arrangement. She informed the students that they would be working at the tables, in small groups, following the lesson's discussion. Using a form of audible self-talk, Ms. Hooks, explained to her class that she wanted to make changes to her previous decision about grouping the students. She then called certain students' names and directed them to sit in small groups at the rear of the room. This process resulted in a purposeful seating arrangement different from the teacher's initial plan.

Teachers' dependence on informal and classroom-based assessments as tools to guide their instructional practices also exposes a dynamic that melds teachers' commitment to teaching and learning and their commitment to students. This amalgamation explains teachers' commitment to continuously vary their instruction according to the learning needs of students. Their persistent nature can be understood through the voice of Ms. Campbell, who proclaimed, "I try not to move on [to another concept] until I see a light bulb," or, in the words of Ms. Adele, who addressed the emotional and academic well-being of students by advising teachers, "Don't give up on them. Never let them quit."

Teachers' dependence on informal and classroom-based assessments is consistent with research on systemic teacher-driven instructional design (Huberman, 1993). While teachers may initiate lessons following an instructional plan, their teaching often becomes artistic through improvisation. When teachers and students come together for instructional purposes, teaching and learning become dynamic. Teachers often have to (re)craft their lessons while "in-action." These artistic instructional movements occur in response to the vicissitudes of students' needs, the availability of resources, as well as the depth and breadth of teachers' instructional repertoires. Yet, such artistry is made difficult in the absence of teachers' ability to engage in skillful and continuous diagnostic judgments regarding the processes of students' learning. Research on the functional units of planning for primary teachers reveals that, "In actually executing the lesson, primary in teachers' minds [is] . . . the task of keeping the lesson flowing and the capitalizing on one of the several opportunities that might emerge [from informal assessment] to introduce, reinforce, or transfer a core skill or content area" (Huberman, 1993, p. 20). In short, as Cohen, Raudenbush, and Ball (2003) explain, teachers and learners are thinking beings who make judgments about each other, their context, and resources. As such, these judgments affect their contextualized actions. More specifically, "Some teachers judge with great care and seek evidence with which they might revise [their instruction], but others judge quickly and with little care. In either event, teachers calibrate instruction to their own view of students' capabilities, and their own capabilities to teach" (p. 132). These judgments and instructional calibrations, particularly when occurring "in-action," are not only informed by, but also make credible the use of classroom-based and informal assessments as providing the pedagogical capacity for engagement in purposeful TLIs.

While all Hillside teachers explicitly expressed value in classroom-based assessments, some questioned the good of externally mandated standardized assessments. Yet, this critical correspondence of formal assessment in no way suggests that teachers ignore the results of standardized tests all together. As an example of how the two converge in the classroom of an individual teacher, Ms. Johnson shared that; "I use classroom assessments for grades, but being cognizant that everything revolves around whether or not your children are proficient on the state test, that's always in the back of my mind." At the building level, however, standardized test results were more likely to be used as a quantifiable measure for the purpose of making school-wide curricular decisions. One reason teachers may have not strongly revered annual (state administered) standardized tests as an instructional guide lies in the fact that these tests were administered in late spring of each year. The results were not reported back to the schools until after the start of the next school year. Hence, teachers have already planned their initial lessons and are well on their way to engaging students in the curriculums by the time the scores are verified by the district and disseminated to the schools. For example, Ms. Jefferson explained:

> We don't usually get the test scores back early enough in the year to use the test information from the previous year; so we have already made decisions . . . by the time the previous years' test results come back.

Simply stated, teachers considered the standardized test scores reported from the previous academic year as lacking an immediate utility, particularly due to the time gap between the testing period and reporting period. Furthermore, two teachers contended that standardized test results only confirm what they already know about students' academic accomplishments (as informed by classroom-based assessments). Nevertheless, district leaders and teachers used students' annual, standardized results during the process of school wide curricular decision-making.

During the time in which the building level administrative role transitioned from Mr. Thachery to Ms. Abbey, Hillside was also in the process of adopting a new reading curriculum. However, students' persistently low performance on standardized reading assessments and teachers' observance of students struggling to phonetically decode words (using informal assessment) were factors leading to the adoption of the school's reading curriculum. Ms. Abbey explained, "We realized though 'in-house' [classroom and site based] assessments that our students needed an explicit and systematic curriculum that would provide the type of structure for decoding and word attack." Ms. Abbey continued to describe the process in which these data influenced school-wide decision: "and after consultation with a couple of people in the district, with the staff, we decided to go ahead with the Harcourt reading curriculum [a textbook series]." Hence, standardized and classroom-based assessments were collaboratively employed in this particular school-wide decision regarding the procurement and utilization of new reading resources. Interesting enough, the school's decision to adopt a new reading curriculum also coincided with the district's test pilot of various reading curriculums.

By most accounts, the teachers shared Ms. Abbey's satisfaction with the current curriculum materials for both mathematics and reading. In fact, Ms. Smith testified, "I feel the curriculum is excellent, excellent. It's what they need right now." Ms. Jefferson clarified that the children were responding well to the language arts curriculum, in part, because it exposed them to new cultural contexts. She explained, "We read a lot of stories about Latin American children; so, they get to see how children in different countries react to situations similar to their own. I think they enjoy the curriculum as a whole." Ms. Campbell agreed that, overall, the math curriculum was effective, because it taught students how to "break down the concepts into numbers that the kids will be easier to work with, like the long division method. It helps them to see the numbers in multiples of tens so that they are easier to work with."

According to Mr. Thachery, the mathematics curriculum was district selected without input at the building level. However, the teachers at Hillside were key players in the district's adoption of the language arts curriculum, as mentioned earlier by Ms. Abbey. Hillside Elementary was one of the school sites within the district chosen to pilot the Harcourt reading series. Ms. Jefferson explained:

> We [teachers] had a lot of input because two teachers were part of the district curriculum committee. They would come back and talk to us to get feedback. I felt comfortable with the choice of our curriculum because it is one that I liked as well. There were teachers, parents and board members on the curriculum committee. They discussed several different curriculums. Our school actually piloted the Harcourt curriculum that was chosen.

The faculty's feedback regarding this series was considered by the district during the adoption process; yet, this decision may simultaneously represent a district's attempt to erase the stigma of low student achievement that has prevailed throughout many of its schools, including Hillside. While teacher's input toward curriculum selection may appear to honor the intellectual acuity of educators at the school level, district oversight for curriculum implementation in relation to teachers' capacity to engage in TLIs may very well undermine their professionalism. As such, the mathematics and reading curriculums (like standardized assessments) represent a district-driven mechanistic strategy of practice (Rowan, 1995). More specifically, the district's adoption of a standardized curriculum may be interpreted as an input control over teachers' instructional decision-making—an input control that could influence teachers' capacity to engage in LTLs and an input control as part of the forward mapping process. Giroux (1988) and Apple (1982, 1986) identify such practice as an attempt to deskill teachers' work. Giroux (1988) explains that, "Teacher decisions about what should be taught, how it might meet the intellectual and cultural needs of students, and how it might be evaluated are rendered unimportant in these packages [packaged curriculums]" (p. 4). In the case of both the reading and mathematics curriculums at Hillside, a certain amount of rigidity restricted decisions around instructional delivery. For example, the Every Day Math curriculum is designed around a paced sequence that dictates the rate at which all teachers should cover the curriculum. Similarly, the Harcourt reading curriculum requires 90-minutes of daily, uninterrupted reading instruction. Paradoxically, teachers identified such restrictions as having an effect on their pedagogical capacity to engage in TLIs. These restrictions also represent a critical correspondence with which the district's effort to reform teachers' instructional practices (i.e., forward mapping that pushes for implementation purity of adopted curriculums in order to ensure pre-determined outcomes) simultaneously challenges teachers' ability to calibrate their instruction while in-action and in response to the learning needs of students.

The Compounding Critical Correspondence of Assessment and Curriculum

While the critical correspondences of assessment and curriculum that impact teachers' engagement in TLIs are distinct and independently unique in many ways, top-down mandates that attempt to increase student achievement result in an intensification as assessment and curriculum converge. For example, the 90-minutes literacy block was designed around weekly units. Each week, teachers were scheduled to introduce a new vocabulary list, to introduce new literary devices such as alliterations (at the intermediate level), and to continue reinforcing reading skills previously covered. A specific thematic narrative, as described earlier by Ms. Jefferson, contextualizes these acts. Yet, by the week's end, teachers were required to bring the text to a close in preparation for a new week. Ms. Jefferson added that even though many children were likely to respond favorably to the content of the curriculum, Harcourt lacked a grammar component for teaching valuable skills tested on the state assessment. Teachers were left to find inventive ways to include grammar instruction outside of the mandated 90-minutes language arts block in order that students might attain the necessary grammar skills needed to pass the state test. Their efforts to do so, however, were restricted due to the pace of the curriculum and the limited about of down time not allocated to prescribed curricular mandates.

The Everyday Mathematics curriculum observed a similar pacing. This curriculum was also organized according to units and, like the Harcourt reading curriculum, was aligned across the district so that theoretically, every day, in every school, and in every classroom, instructional practices should be focused on a particular range of skills. Because of the pacing, teachers were forced to make strategic decisions about their instructional practices in accordance with the curricular designs. Ms. Campbell explained:

> We have a chart that indicates what lessons should be taught by the end of each month. Also, each lesson is broken down into sections. There is a specific time requirement for each section. For instance, the mental math and the math message should take only ten to fifteen minutes, and the whole meat of the lesson, teaching a new concept, should take forty-five. To do the math boxes and to play the math games that should take another fifteen to twenty minutes. So, we have to make sure that we stay with the pacing. Do we get through everything in every lesson? No!

Curricular and assessment demands converged as Hillside (and the district) attempted to improve student achievement scores on the state exam by aligning its curriculums with specific skills to be tested on the exam. Assessing the condition from an administrator's perspective, Ms. Abbey explained that while she believed that the Hillside student population might benefit from supplemental materials that may also increase their learning, liberties for her to make curricular decisions at the building level were narrowed by a (national/ state/district) charge to raise student performance outcomes on the state test. Because of chronic low-test scores, Ms. Abbey also pondered:

> We need to do some of the alignment that some of the other districts have done in terms of finding the core of the curriculum, what has to be taught, what children must know, and what they need to know . . . pulling out the redundancies and the parts of the curriculum that just don't have [measurable] impact, or that have the same impact.

Perhaps Ms. Abbey's fledging principalship and her limited skills for brokering a buffer between teachers' capacity for TLIs and the district's heavy-handed gavel for pounding out a curricular and instructional sentencing are to blame for the rigid reading programming. Whatever the case, the limits of the curriculums to address the full range of the essential elements necessary for students' learning were not lost among the Hillside educators. As well, the inept ability to effect certain curricular changes beyond the demands of the state test was felt at all levels of the school, among teachers and the principal alike. Ms. Campbell described how the emphasis on alignment between the curriculum (pace and content) and the state test affected her teaching of mathematics:

> We have to pick and choose and decide where we are going to stop. But the main components of the lessons we need to cover. Some things are sent home for homework. For example, if it is a review, if the math boxes are a review, then we will give it to them for homework.

What is represented in this alignment model is a technical rational approach to schooling, one that reduces teachers' curricular decision making in a significant way. As demonstrated in Ms. Campbell's experience, the teachers' curricular and instructional decisions are limited by bureaucratic demands to align the curriculums and his/her work around particular skill sets identified on a high stakes assessment—the state test. Teachers are prevented from maximizing their intellectual or professional capacity to question what students should know and learn (Robertson, 1996; Giroux, 1988) beyond the constraints of standardized testing. This technical rational model perpetuates schooling as a system that values certain bodies of knowledge over others and reduces teachers' role to that of a technocratic worker whose instructional responsibility is to transmit the knowledge and skills that can be aligned between the curriculums and the state accountability measurement. Within this system, standardized tests operate as a control mechanism (Rowan 1995), disciplinary power (Collins, 2009), and a panopticon of surveillance (Foucault, 1979; Bushnell, 2003) that monitor, measure, and make teachers accountable for a certain level of instructional efficiency. Hence, curricular alignment is reduced to a practice of coordinating instructional content and practices with accountability demands. Curricular alignment of this sort produces a critical correspondence, which appears to restrict teachers' capacity for engagement in TLIs as the temptation not to "teach to the test" grows ever so challenging. Ms. Day explained, "You're not supposed to teach to the test, but that's how you are evaluated. So, the choice is difficult."

Curriculums and TLIs
By exposing the intensified critical correspondences of both the mathematics and reading curriculums, what emerges is an understanding that curriculums (though possibly supported by research on cognitive learning and effective teaching practices) often evolve from certain "zones of wishful thinking" (Hill & Celio, 1998). As such, assumptions are made about effective implementation and anticipated outcomes. Top-down policies assume that policymakers control the organizational, political, and technical processes that affect implementation (Elmore, 1979). Textbook writers tend to make similar assumptions about the

contexts of schools. Even when textbooks and curriculums are designed in response to educational debates such as culturally sensitive instruction for minorities versus teaching a common culture (Delpit, 1995; Smith-Maddox, 1998; Nieto, 1997) and whole language versus phonics (Dahl, Scharer, Lawson & Grogan, 1999; Manning & Kamii, 2000; Hempenstall, 2005), certain generalizations about the contexts of schools prevail, particularly for inner-city, urban schools like Hillside. More specifically, the assumptions are that children come to school ready to learn and that students come from homes in which there are instructionally supportive structures. These assumptions reflect a hegemonic ideology that traditionally shapes not only the design of public policies, but also educational policies that are quick to implicate teachers and schools with significant blame for low student achievement on test scores.

As found in the context of Hillside, textbook series adopted by districts are often translated into the core curriculums of many schools. Cohen et al. (2003) contend that, "The designers and publishers of materials also frame content to manage the environments of instruction, as when texts intended for sale in Southern states fail to mention evolution" (p. 127). Yet, designers and publishers simultaneously make erroneous assumptions about the contexts of schools. These assumptions are often formed from generalized data about schools and present schools with a technical recipe for instructional delivery—a recipe that purports academic success for all children, as long as teachers follow the teacher's manuals. Here again, such claims move teachers into a position of blame when achievement scores do not rise.

In an attempt to shape and account for the context of schools, textbook and curriculum architects are unable to predict *all* contextual variables that affect teaching and learning (e.g. the social and emotional needs and academic readiness of students). This inability to predict contextualized variables represents an inherent critical correspondence of curriculums. The teachers at Hillside identified several critical correspondences of curriculum that impact their engagement in TLIs. These critical correspondences problematize the textbook driven curriculums that assume: (1) students are intrinsically motivated to learn and will find relevance in the proposed curricular content; (2) students are academically ready to engage the curriculums; and (3) students will receive instructional support/reinforcement at home.

Curriculums and Students' Motivation
While Ms. Jefferson highlighted the reading curriculum's attention to culturally diverse representations of children as a plus, she spoke from a singular perspective. For her, the children were responding well to the curriculum, in part because of its attention to diverse cultural representations. However, other teachers at Hillside took notice that many children appeared to lack a fair amount of intrinsic motivation. Like Ms. Abbey, many teachers and the broader public tend to believe that education is for the purpose of bettering one's life

(Mathews, 1996; Hirschland & Steinmo, 2003), but several Hillside teachers explained that numerous children seem not share this same belief. Ms. Johnson declared, "We have a lot of kids who don't place any value on education. They don't understand its importance." It has been her experience that many students do not see education as a valuable investment. For Ms. Johnson, children's value of education aligned not with the ideals promoted by teachers inside the school but with their own communities and certain images promoted by popular culture. She pointed to pop icons as an example of one motivating force for children. Ms. Johnson explained how she understood the ways in which children were reading the world:

> We [educators] are up against great odds. Society too, doesn't place a whole lot of importance on education. The kids see sports stars and rap stars who don't speak correct English. So "why do I need to speak correct English because they don't? Look! They are driving around in a Hummer and they have gold chains, and I'm getting me some of those too." So, we are up against a public force.

Ms. Johnson, who taught mathematics for her grade level, admitted that her students' lack of intrinsic motivation to learn both impeded and provided capacity for engagement in TLIs. She attested that motivating students—to work independently, to find joy in solving mathematical challenges through intellectual struggle—was an everyday challenge. As an example, she reported that the students in her classroom would become frustrated when unable to quickly solve problems. They would begin to bemoan the assignments and the practices of schooling. Yet, because of their lack of intrinsic motivation, she must continually seek ways to stimulate their interests for learning through engagement in TLIs.

As stated earlier, contradictions also occur across classrooms. These contradictions highlight the individual perspectives of teachers. For Ms. Adele, popular culture was viewed as an instructional tool with the potential for motivating students and for engaging in a particular TLI. She explained that innovative teaching "comes from using techniques relevant to children." For example:

> Their world is not the same as ours was. And you have to understand that. If you are using something they see on TV as the symbols in your math problems, that's innovative. They become interested. And, I know we don't like to focus everything on TV, but I'm saying you've got to make lessons relevant to them. If not, it's not going to make any sense to them.

Similarly, in the case of Ms. Campbell, she had been able to achieve a certain level of success toward motivating students' capacity for intellectual struggle. Ms. Campbell explained that independent learning and student driven mathematical deliberations were made possible through explicit expectations and continuous practice. She stated that students have to practice making their ideas public. Early in the school year, she informs the students of the classroom expectations she has set and provides structured time for students to practice explaining their answers to the whole class while others practice listening without giggling or interrupting. While occurring infrequently, she described how practice, motivation, and learning come together as an ideal:

> For instance when we were doing problem solving one day, practicing for the state assessment, I had one student explain what she did and why she did it. Her explanation was a little off. So, even before I asked a question, one of the students asked her to explain herself a little more. They didn't understand what she was saying. So when she repeated again, the gentleman caught her mistake and corrected her. And she wasn't upset about the correction because of how he said it. And when he did that, she said, "OK! I understand, I meant da, da, da, da, da" and corrected herself. Then he chimed in "you could have also done this" and gave another example. So, for that moment, I was out of the equation, and it was the two students talking about their strategies of a certain problem. That's when you know they've got it, when they are able to explain and have a discussion about a problem.

These acts of deliberation represent the actualization of one teacher's anticipated outcomes of a TLI that promotes students' engagement in intellectual struggle. Cohen et al., (2003) clarify that deliberations, like the one demonstrated above, advance the teaching and learning process because "students who have learned to reflect on their ideas, listen carefully, and express themselves clearly are likely to make better use of materials, teachers, and other students' work. They also are likely to make it easier for other students and teachers to use their work [as well]" (p. 125). Yet, Ms. Campbell was sure that such acts would not occur by fiat or in the absence of routine practice—practice for public reflection on one's thought processes and practice for active listening and the engagement of classmates' ideas. She also made clear that this type of deliberation occurred as a result of a change in her teaching practices over time. Ms. Campbell explained that not only must students learn the process of deliberation, but only over time and through self-discipline had she come to teach in a way that promotes intellectual struggle through independent and group problem solving. Only over time have her instructional practices changed. Only over time had she become skilled and comfortable enough to reduce teacher talk for the purpose of guiding students to engage in acts of deliberation. This process defines a TLI that occurred as one teacher's knowledge and skills developed, in due course. This example reflects the experience of an individual teacher who modified her instructional practices (i.e., teacher talk) in order to motivate students to think deeply about mathematics and to encourage them to struggle intellectually through a practice of classroom deliberation. Ms. Campbell did add, however, that even before students' intellectual investment could be garnered, much time was needed for them to develop confidence and to begin to trust their own abilities. She also made it known that much of her work was frontloaded with helping students to listen earnestly to one another, without judgments and the teasing of one another when mistakes or trepidations were rendered.

Nurturant Relationships and Students' Motivation

While, teachers expressed that many students were not necessarily motivated by the textbook designed curriculums, their commitment to and nurturant relationships with students may have functioned as an immediate motivating force for children (i.e., a form of pedagogical capacity for engagement in TLIs). For a majority of teachers, their nurturant interactions with students were intentional and demonstrate their commitment to meeting students' diverse (academic, social, and emotional) learning needs. Their interactions were deliberate attempts to engage students in the learning process. Ms. Adele explained that she continuously encourages students to always do their best. For her, a teacher should interact with children, thereby creating an active classroom. Ms. Adele emoted:

> You can't be behind a desk and interact with your children in order to accomplish what they need. They need reinforcement. They need to see a teacher who is looking and praising and positively reinforcing and correcting and saying, "No, don't say you can't. No, you can do better. Yes, you can. Ok, let's see it. Is that your best?" I'm constantly questioning the children about what they are doing, "Is that the best you can do?" And they are honest. They'll look at you and they will say, "No." I'll say, "Don't we always say we will do our very best?" [The student replies,] "Uhu." And, they will try again. You have to keep encouraging them. You have to keep pushing them. They don't have a lot of confidence in themselves. And, they don't have a lot of joy for learning. And, that's what they need to have. They need to have that enthusiasm. And it's a round of applause if you get something right. And "Can you believe you did that!" It has to be about an excitement for what you are learning. And, I don't care how old you are, learning has to be a goal in and of itself, . . . supported by a desire to learn.

While their styles are varied, Ms. Lenora also exhibited a fervent commitment for motivating students to learn. In her mathematics class, students were expected to come to class prepared and to actively participate in each lesson. Ms. Lenora persistently challenged students to explain their work on paper (in writing) and verbally, during class sessions. She questions, "I want to know how you got the answer?" "Did anyone solve the problem in a different way?" And she rephrases, "How would you figure this problem out?" No one in her class is given the opportunity to hide behind mindless excuses. Making examples of children who fail to complete required homework assignment(s), Ms. Lenora further advances her standard of engagement. She gives a gentle directive to work the problem(s) out now, in class. She even reassigns tasks for homework a second time.

Research on cultural and environmental factors that influence African American students' academic performance buttresses the judgments of these teachers—expressions that teachers must care enough to express high expectations and encouragement. Delpit (1995) postulates that African American students often understand authority as a teacher's ability to earn their respect by controlling the classroom environment, believing that students can learn and by "pushing" them to succeed academically. Wilson and Corbett's (2001) research on minority, inner-city, urban students reveals that students respect teachers who not only modify their instruction so that lessons are meaningful, but who also hold and make known their high expectations for students' engagement and achievement. Thus, authority and encouragement, in this regard, connote caring teachers and a certain level of teacher efficacy/quality. The assertion of authority and encouragement within the classroom acts as a TLI that motivates students to learn. Noguera (2003b) draws conclusions based on his own research (and others') with African American students to posit that students' perceptions of and feelings about their teachers influence their academic performance. More specifically, "If [African American] students do not believe that their teachers care about them and are actively concerned about their academic performance, the likelihood that they will succeed is greatly reduced" (p. 119).

Curriculums and Students' Academic Readiness
Besides assuming that students will automatically find curriculums intriguing, stimulating, and relevant, textbook driven curricular architects often take for granted that students entering a grade level are able to engage the curriculums at that level. This is not to take away from the fact that classroom teachers, administrators, and anyone familiar with the American educational system understands that each school year begins with a review of previously learned concepts, skills, and classroom routines. More savvy textbook driven curriculums are even designed on spiral models that attempt to accommodate students who might need additional help by routinely reviewing previously introduced concepts. Yet, by and large, the assumption is made that third graders read within a third grade range. Herein lies a critical correspondence that some teachers experienced on a regular basis. Campbell explained that:

> A lot of the curriculum is written assuming that student come to school or come to this grade level with certain background knowledge and experiences. But with the population that we are working with, the kids don't have a lot of that background. So, a lot of times I have to go backwards and build that background before we can move forward.

She clarified that not only do many students lack knowledge of basic skills, but also the cultural competency needed to engage certain texts. In response, teachers at Hillside frequently engaged in TLIs that set out to build students' cultural competency by making instruction relevant to their lived experiences or by coaxing students to extend their imaginations beyond their immediate, physical surroundings. For example, when reading a story about a young man traversing the snowy mountains (during a wintry storm) while being pulled on a sled by a dog, Ms. Jefferson asked students, "Can you imagine what's going on? What does it look like? Close your eyes and think about this." As I observed classrooms, it became apparent that other teachers often took a teacher on the stage instructional approach to introducing and reviewing basic skills, particularly at the primary level. These lessons were generally teacher directed. The teachers instructed students to stay together by putting their finger on a particular problem in their drill book. The students individually provided an answer to a problem. The teachers wrote the correct answer on the board and directed the children to do the same in their books, leaving no room for error. While such a practice may not appear creative, direct instruction may be classified as a TLI to the extent that the collective, and generally lower ordered learning needs of students are met.

Delpit (1995) explains that African American children often struggle with curriculums because of a lack of cultural competency and an unfamiliarity with the codes of power from which progressive education is fashioned. She provides an example in which students who do not come to school primed to engage in curriculums are quickly labeled remedial. Hence, teachers at Hillside, in order to meet the academic needs of students, have to find ways to teach children basic (lower order) skills (e.g., through direct instruction) and to generate a level of cultural competency while simultaneously preparing them for higher ordered and critical thinking literacy(ies).

Ms. Williams, who taught for many years in non-minority and middle-class schools, explained how her teaching had changed in order to teach even the most basic of skills:

> In my other building [of middle class White students] I would be able to teach a lesson differently, whereas here I recognized the need for a lot of repetition and the use of chants. They learn a lot better in this environment through repetition and always reviewing. In the other building I might have had to review a skill once or twice and children were able to retain information, whereas here that is not case.

She further explained how working at Hillside has been an investment in the expansion of her teaching repertoire (i.e., the development of knowledge and skills that provide the capacity for engagement in TLIs): "Now, I have bettered my teaching because of this environment. Here I am learning different teaching styles."

As mentioned earlier, teachers' engagement in TLIs is further intensified by the paced sequence of both the Every Day Math and Harcourt curriculums.

Several teachers expressed concern with their abilities to adequately address students' learning needs while simultaneously maintaining an instructional pace equal to curricular demands. Again, textbook and curriculum architects assume that children at each grade level come to school ready to engage the curriculum at that level. Ms. Campbell critiqued the Everyday Math curriculum:

> I don't feel that it provides enough repetition with certain things, the practice and drill that our kids need and the basics like multiplication, subtraction—borrowing and trading. And I also know that other teachers in the district have that same complaint. So, we have to use other supplements that provide the repetition.

She and other teachers expressed a discomfort with the curriculums' paced sequence. Ms. Campbell reiterated how students' lack of background knowledge influences the rhythm of her teaching and engagement in TLIs:

> Often I see they have no prior knowledge of anything that I am talking about, that the book says that they should. That's when I know that I have to go back and review some things just so we can get to the point where the book wants us, so that we can move on. So, a lot of times, yes, we fall behind [in the paced schedule]. So I have to steal time from other things like Social Studies and checking the homework.

These responses represent teachers' critical read of curricular pacing as a practice that impedes student learning in relation to their academic readiness. These responses illustrate the ways in which teachers modify their instructional routines in order to accommodate the learning needs of their students.

Ms. Abbey reported that several intermediate level teachers had begun to question the efficacy of the curriculums' pace. Yet, due to district demands, she has encouraged them to follow the curriculums as designed. By "stealing" time away from other content areas to focus on the school's curricular mantra of mathematics and reading, teachers purposefully prioritized their engagement in TLIs according to those practices that are rewarded (Robertson, 1996) by school administrators and district leaders. Stated differently, they intentionally focused on concepts and content areas to be assessed on the state test while ignoring others as a practice that promises to raise students' achievement on this assessment.

Still, teachers' deep concern for the emotional well-being of students permeated their daily work. An informal dialogue with two primary teachers during their lunchtime revealed that the curricular pacing challenged their ethical/moral beliefs about teaching and learning—beliefs steeped in an ethic of care (Gillian, 1982; Noddings, 1992). These teachers (in the presence of a university volunteer and a student teacher) verbalized their common concern for the trickle-down effect of high stakes testing, its influence on curricular design, and the emotional well-being of their students. They discussed their perceived disconnect between the reading and mathematics curriculums, their pacing, and the academic readiness of many students. Ms. Adele and Ms. Smith questioned the developmental appropriateness of such pacing. They explained that only a small number of students were able to continuously demonstrate mastery of standards at the rate demanded by the paced curriculums. Yet, these teachers made clear that they were required to press forward with instruction and to move on to the next lesson, even though far too many students continued to struggle with partially learned standards and skills from previous lessons. What results is a mass of low-performing students who become frustrated from a lack of success. In order to compensate for students' frustrations, these teachers explained that they persistently praise students for the smallest of achievements. They continuously remind students of the progress they have made, individually and collectively. Herein lies an example of engagement (i.e., thinking, talking, and doing) in a TLI in which teachers discuss and reflect on the calibration of their instructional/classroom practices in response to their understanding of the critical correspondences between the paced curriculums and the learning needs of students.

Curriculums and Students' Instructionally Supportive Home Life
Not unlike other textbook driven curriculums, the teacher's guide for both the Every Day Math and Harcourt reading series provide teachers with certain suggestions regarding the assignment of homework tasks. Textbook architects, teachers, and anyone who has attended school understand homework as a common practice of schooling. This understanding portrays homework as an instructional tool that advances students' learning through repetition and practice at home, outside of the regular school day. This understanding also harbors the assumption that homework assignments function as a bridge between the classroom and home. What resonates in the minds of many Americans, particularly with respect to children at the elementary level, are memories and hopes of parents sitting with their children at the kitchen table assisting them with some project or assignment.

Research in this area reveals positive correlations between parents' involvement and student achievement (U.S. Department of Education, 2001). Yet, this research is broad and often fails to make explicit the meanings and functions of parental involvement (Lawson, 2003; Bailey, 2002). Also, research on parental involvement varies by race, ethnicity, class, and even cultural norms. Moreover, research on low-income communities explains that parental involvement is often non-existent or greatly strained (Noguera, 2003; Lawson, 2003; Knight, 2003).

Teachers at Hillside explained that parental involvement with homework directly affected their pedagogical capacity to engage in TLIs. They explained that many students lacked the needed assistance to complete homework assignments—assistance that would make their jobs easier (Lawson, 2003). They also contributed limited parental involvement to socioeconomic markers. For example, when asked to reflect on one factor that influences her work at Hillside, Ms. Campbell responded: "The population that I have to deal with, knowing that a majority of the children are from low-income families." She continued:

> Unfortunately a lot of the parents may not work with the children as we would like them to, particularly with their homework. I have asked many students if there is someone at home to help them with their homework or to help them with their multiplication facts. And many times, the students will say no.

Ms. Campbell compared Hillside's context to other schools by explaining what researchers and community organizers have been saying all along that "At many of the other schools of different economic[ly secure] backgrounds where the parents are more involved, you see a big difference."

Though not made explicit, what is captured in this statement is an awareness that schools and families are connected. In fact, the 2008 principal of the year for St. Louis Public Schools who has made tremendous strides at building bridges between his high school and the surrounding community explains that "A school is only as healthy as the community it serves" (Terry Houston, Personal Communications, May 7, 2008). The teachers of Hillside spoke of the connection(s) between the school and families as joined by a narrow pathway that is open in only one direction. Students cross this pathway, homework pages cross this pathway, and messages to parents cross this pathway. Conveyed in Ms. Campbell's statements (and others to follow) is a sentiment that the school is overwhelming impacted by family issues (and the community in which students live) that affect students' learning. Conversely, informal conversations between teachers depicted families as being unmoved by the steps teachers take to advance children's academic growth. As I observed the comings and goings and interactions among parents and school officials, it became abundantly clear that, more often than not, parents would visit the school in response to behavioral problems of their children, or with concern to issues in which a parent perceived mistreatment on their child's behalf. And, with the exception of the one parent who coordinated tutors for the reading center, and another parent who worked as a classroom aide in one of the primary level classrooms, a parent visiting the school to discuss their children's grades and/or academic progress was a sight rarely seen.

Teachers sensed that their work was intensified by a school-family connection that failed to fully support students' academic advancement. Only one teacher made mention of inroads taken by the school to bridge the relations between Hillside and the community as a means to help parents to more fully assist students with homework assignments. Ms. Jefferson elaborated:

I know that for a lot of parents it is difficult [to help their children with home-work] because they don't understand our math curriculum, for instance. But, we have offered numerous parent workshops on how to provide support at home. I don't think many of our parents take advantage of what's out there for them to use.

What was missing from this argument and dialogues with teachers, howev-er, was a critical questioning of what actions Hillside might have taken to repair the pathway between the school and families in order to ensure that communica-tion, problem solving, instructional support for students, and collaboration were navigated in both directions. Yet, research demonstrates that teachers tend to receive limited, if any, training in communicating with families, particularly regarding homework tasks (Bryan, Burstein & Bryan, 2001; Bailey, 2002). Related research on the types of knowledge taught in leadership preparation programs reveals that principals too are less likely prepared to develop school-parent and community relationships in comparison to other knowledge domains recognized among highly effective school leaders (Orr & Easley, 2009). Even still, roles for parent participation tend to be defined by the schools, in the absence of collaboration with parents.

The notion of a healthy school-family relationship (in which parents assist their children with homework assignments) emerged as a critical issue as Hillside teachers began to admit that parents may very well struggle to under-stand the tenets of the new Every Day Math curriculum. When asked, "Because the math curriculum is taught differently [than what parents are accustomed to leaning mathematics], do you think this poses a problem for parents being able to assist their children at home?" Ms. Campbell candidly responded:

Yes! Especially with some of the algorithms and methods of how to solve prob-lems. Now that does pose a problem, but . . . parents . . . [could] just reinforce the basic facts that do not change—the multiplication, adding and subtracting—because everything in the curriculum is based upon knowing these basic facts. So if the kids have help at home learning the basic facts, then all the other con-cepts that we are teaching will be made easier for the kids to understand.

Yet, Ms. Johnson problematized the issue even further, adding that, "Some parents are illiterate. Most parents didn't even graduate high school." These perspectives raised a concern about parents' ability to provide instructional support at home due to their own educational inadequacies. Though contrary to the norm in which teachers often blame low-income and African American parents for their children's poor academic achievement (Thompson, 2003), the teachers of Hillside fell short of blaming parent as being apathetic. They did not believe that the parents inherently do not care about their children. However, they did draw a correlation between the home and students' value of education as well as students' completion of homework assignments. For example, during a particular primary grade level meeting, teachers' revealed their collective thoughts about homework and parental support. For this group of teachers, homework assignments were calibrated/designed in a unique manner according to the perceived characteristics of their students' collective home support structure. Homework assignments were designed to reinforce skills that students had already been taught in class. Homework was designed for repetition and drill. Homework was designed in such a way that students would need little assistance. During the meeting, one teacher explained to Ms. Abbey and the Reading ITL that students tend not to return homework and that when returned, the work is frequently overrun with errors. Ms. Johnson clarified how this reality affected her work. She did not always assume that children would have homework support, so she deliberately planned instructional time to reinforce skills that would normally have occurred through homework assignments outside of class. She further explained her thinking behind this particular TLI:

> I assume that any learning that needs to take place is going to happen here in the school. For example, our math curriculum has what are called home links that are sent home. They turn into small projects where students need to collect things such newspapers or old boxes to talk about numbers, weights and balances and whatever is on the boxes. I tried that in years past and it doesn't work because you will have one or two students who are actually participating in the home component that they need to finish the lesson in class. So anything that requires assistance at home, I do kind of shy away from because I know from experience that it won't be completed. I just assume that any learning that is going to go on is going to happen here. And, if a student does have parents who are willing to help and will work with them, then that's just a bonus.

This data affirms the critical correspondence of textbook designed curriculums which assume that students automatically receive instructional support outside of the school and highlights how teachers might modify their instructional practices accordingly.

As recognized by Ms. Johnson's comment, parental involvement that takes place within some homes was not completely lost on teachers. In fact, their evaluation of the limited parental involvement noted within their school was consistent with other research in this area. This research explains that even though many conditions of low-income, inner-city, urban communities burden parental involvement, such participation, when occurring, does positively impact students' academic success (Ascher, 1988; Wilson & Allen, 1987). Ms. Abbey described the home life of many Hillside children in which the parents are "missing in action" and that many grandparents have taken charge of rearing their grandchildren. She continued, letting it be known that many parents are so preoccupied by their own personal crises that they often neglect paying attention to their children's involvement in school. Describing a condition in which families are cut off from the formal economic structure and have reverted to an informal economic structure (Noguera, 2003), Ms. Jefferson added that "We have a lot of children who come from single family homes, where parents aren't working or they are doing things of the illegal sort to make money." Yet she and Ms. Campbell both explained that for those students who received assistance with homework, their growth and understanding of the lessons' content were obvious. Ms. Jefferson argued that these students, at minimum, were able to clearly articulate where they are struggling and in what ways they needed additional help from teachers. She also pointed to other avenues for instructional support attained by students outside of school. These consisted of after school programs, community programs, and churches.

Discussion

What can be extrapolated from these perspectives is that teachers' attempts to engage in TLIs are made dynamic by the policy demands of forward mapping regarding assessment and curriculum. Their work is challenged by contradictory perspectives—one that values governance over teachers' practices for the purpose of implementation purity versus one that values teachers' use of professional decision making about teaching and learning as guided by teachers' broad assessments of students' learning needs such as their readiness and motivational levels. Hence, their work is affected by conditions outside of the school, outside of the classroom, and beyond the design of policy. Such is the critical correspondence of policy driven school reform.

In order for them to engage in TLIs, teachers have to uncover the immediate and ever-changing needs of students and reinterpret curricular demands in relation to the dispositions of students, resources, their own instructional repertoires, and other environmental factors. Teaching is more than following procedures for assessment or a textbook driven curriculum guide. Cohen et al. (2003) explain that, "Teaching is what teachers do, say, and think with learners, concerning content, in particular organizations and other environments, in time" (p. 124). In order for teachers to motivate students, they must go beyond the curriculum. They must meet students where they are. This chapter reveals that teachers must first recognize the basic needs of students—a need for motivation and a need for academic readiness to engage in policy driven, high stakes instruction. These needs are uncovered and accommodated as a result of teachers' skillful and continuous assessment of students' progress throughout the teaching and learning process.

Bailey (2002) and others (e.g., Comer & Haynes, 1991) suggest that teachers support student learning by engaging parents in the learning process. This means understanding what parents value about education, providing structures by which teachers and parents can (co)construct homework modules, and providing opportunities for parents to help out in classrooms. Yet, teachers' capacity to engage parents in meaningful ways is made difficult by their limited preparation and know-how—skills that are rarely addressed during their pre-service experiences and skills that are under supported through in-service trainings that are aligned with strategic plans for strong classroom-family relationships through the organization.

Returning to the notion of a one directional pathway between the community and school, Mathews (1996) argues that good schools are the roots of good communities and a good country. He continues to stress that communities are "an essential source of 'social capital,' a necessary form of reinforcement from outside of the school that encourages students to learn" (p. 6). This means that schools and communities are intricately connected. Yet, many low-income African American students living in the inner-city, like the Hillside children, live in communities marred by few resources, racial isolation, limited local capital and political influence, crime, violence, drugs, poor public health, teenage childbirth, and intergenerational poverty (Cooper & Jordan, 2003; Kozol, 1991; Noguera, 2003b). A lack of social capital burdens inner-city, urban communities' potential to access the resources of social networks like schools (Noguera, 2003; Easley, 2009). When parents know how to make the system work on behalf of their children, the potential for academic success rises. For most low-income, poorly educated, inner-city families such know-how (social capital) is limited or nonexistent.

These conditions suggest that the work needed to leave no child behind for the full development of their and academic potentials extends beyond the reach of forward mapping and policy driven (assessments/curriculums) reforms, far beyond the classroom and even the school. These findings are a reminder that schools exist within and are responsive to larger sociopolitical systems such as school districts and local communities (Sarason, 1990, Norguera, 2003). These findings demonstrate that schools do not exist in a vacuum, thereby troubling technical-rationale approaches to school reform—approaches that seek to make rationale the context of school and schoolings through the application of certain input and output control mechanisms. Particularly for low-performing schools that serve low-income, minority, and politically disconnected families, serious discussions are needed to better understand how communities, districts, and schools might collectively author a cohesive agenda that is sensitive to the multiple realities of all stakeholders. This means engaging students, teachers, school/district administrators, parents, community leaders, and policy architects in public deliberations regarding the contextual critical correspondences of educational policies and the process of schooling (i.e., school-family-community relations, assessment, curriculum, the needs of students, the pedagogical capacity for teachers' engagement in TLIs, etc.). Yet, these deliberations will do little to meet this aim in the absence of democratic dialogue in which stakeholders take time to genuinely listen to each other, to "suspend assumptions and enter into a genuine 'thinking together'" (Senge, 1990, p. 10). Simultaneously, such deliberations will do little good in the absence of a system of reciprocal accountability (Goldstein et al. 1998; Easley, 2005) in which all stakeholders are made responsible for fulfilling their role in the reform efforts and in which passing the blame exists no more.

Chapter Five
Context and Collaboration as Pedagogical Capacity

One of the theories-of-action underlying the reconstitution of schools (like Hillside) is the assertion that new working conditions will evolve from the hiring of more talented and committed teachers and administrators, and that these new conditions will be characterized by a high level of collaboration (Malen et al., 2002). Mr. Thachery also believed in the need for a collaborative and collegial culture among teachers. Hargreaves (1994) contends that collaboration and collegiality are the cornerstones of school improvement and are "fruitful strategies for fostering teacher development" (p. 186). For a reconstituted school like Hillside, which reopened with a faculty of 75% fledgling teachers, building a new culture becomes important. Because many of the newly hired teachers had less than three years of experience, it is easy to conceive collaboration as an important function of staff development. As Mr. Thachery explained: "Most teachers see themselves as teachers of an individual class. I wanted teachers to start thinking about a collective responsibility for all of the kids in a particular grade level." In order for this to be achieved, he conceptualized collaboration as both a structural and cultural norm for fostering teacher development. Such a plan supports the notion of engagement in teaching and learning innovations (TLIs) to the extent that teachers are expected to collaboratively cogitate and converse about the multiple ways in which they might modify their instructional and classroom practices to meet the diverse learning needs of students. Mr. Thachery continued:

> I built into the schedule a double planning period. Instead of having [individual planning] time scheduled for thirty minutes for five days a week, such time would occur two or three days a week, across the school. I built into their schedule at each grade level one day of a double planning period. That meant they got an extra preparation period a week for the purpose of discussing instructional issues. I didn't want them talking about planning field trips and things like that. It was devoted to data analysis, using [student] data[1] to plan lessons. It was to get feedback and to allow the time to do observations in other classrooms or other schools. It was an opportunity for me to bring in other people to work with them around instructional issues.

While Mr. Thachery held a high regard for collaboration and collegiality as factors of teacher development, teachers' ways of understanding the context of their work did not necessarily align with those of administrators. Furthermore, since the implementation of reconstitution, many changes had shaped and altered the context of Hillside and the function of collaboration. Two important changes have been the hire of a new, first-time principal as well as the federal enactment and implementation of the No Child Left Behind Act of 2001. During my visit to the school, the teachers at Hillside expressed their individual and collective interpretations of how a changing context impacts their collaborative ties and the ways in which the double planning sessions, over time, had influenced their capacity to engage in teaching TLIs. This chapter explores these interpretations.

Collaboration and the Double Planning Period

Ms. Smith recalled her excitement in knowing that nearly everyone in the re-constituted school would be new, thereby representing a fresh start. She identified both the notion of a fresh start and Mr. Thachery's clear vision for the school as factors motivating her to apply for a teaching position at Hillside. Ms. Smith described the first years of reconstitution: "It was tough in the beginning, but everybody did have a lot of energy and enthusiasm. And I think it worked out well. We came together as a team, and that's really what was important." However, while energy, enthusiasm, and a principal's vision are important, they independently will not bring about coherence among teachers—the coherence needed to define teams as collaborative and collegial relationships. Problematizing this issue even further, Rosenholz (1991) explains that:

> Although principals may initially define school reality as collaborative, its momentum most likely will flag without ongoing teacher support. That is, teacher collaboration is unlikely to stand in the shadow of one powerful actor alone. Instead, norms of collaboration tend to maintain themselves through daily activities led by those who possess such inclinations. (p. 64)

Hence, collaborative relationships among teachers need both the leadership of principals and the collective energy of its members. Mr. Thachery envisioned collaboration as a vehicle for fostering staff development practices that would raise student achievement. Fullan (2001) warns, however, that such vision and energies should focus on the right things lest they end up producing powerfully wrong results. While a focus on learning is paramount to school effectiveness and student success, Knapp, Copland, and Talbert (2003) explain that the challenge for leaders is to establish a collective focus on learning without compromises that dilute the agenda. By simultaneously attending to too many competing interests and faddishly oscillating from innovation to innovation, the capacity for school effectiveness is diminished. Innovation overload is a phenomenon commonly recognized as a leading cause of teacher burnout and institutional ineptitude.

For the teachers at Hillside, the double planning period represented specific functions; yet, these representations varied historically. Several teachers explained that during the early stages of reconstitution, the double planning periods were more than moments for instructional preparation. They represented guaranteed times during the week in which teachers could commune, talk about instruction, and learn from each other (i.e., a formalized capacity building structure for the engagement in TLIs). When asked, "How were the double planning sessions structured when you first came to Hillside and how were they meaningful?" Ms. Lenora elaborated:

> It wasn't just a double planning, but we would have professional development sessions prior to our double planning. So that when we met for the double planning, we would have specific things that we would have to work on to incorporate into our classes. So, there was a direction because the double planning was tied into the professional development. Like when we first adopted the Waterford program [a skills enrichment computer based program for children], we had the training first, and we used the double planning to decide how we were going to use it in the classroom. We talked about different ways to incorporate it [according to the learning needs of students].

These sessions were used to make meaning of new information, as is exemplified in Ms. Lenora's response. According to Brown & Duguid (2000), information is mechanical until it becomes knowledge though "social life." Others concur (Polyni, 1958, 1966; Nonaka & Takeuchi, 1995; Al-Hawamdeh, 2002) that explicit knowledge, or information, is translated into tacit knowledge such as skills and competencies when people interact among themselves and with the environment. Ms. Lenora's statement illustrates a social context in which teachers collaborated about the use of newly acquired information (e.g., the Waterford computer program) within a particular school, within particular classrooms, and with a focus on learning for particular students. For the teachers at Hillside, these early double planning sessions represented a network for intellectual engagement about their work context in relation to their TLIs. They also used these sessions to discuss information presented during staff development sessions. Such networks transform the meaning of "drive-by" staff development sessions in which teachers are made the objects of experts' presentations. In this regard, they become networks for teacher development as information is made into knowledge through meaningful dialogue—dialogue that is teacher directed and teacher owned.

What significantly resonated with several teachers is that these meetings were context specific. Ms. Day recalled that, when instructional initiatives were introduced, teachers were allowed to experiment with the new information in their own classrooms and with real students before discussing their responses during the double planning sessions. For her, these meetings were student centered to the degree that they focused on student learning and these meeting were data driven. Ms. Day explained that instructional decisions were made based on teacher driven and teacher-tested data regarding "what worked with our children." These interpretations bring into focus teachers' voices and teachers' insider understanding of their work context, thereby revealing that teachers may hold fast to their unique interpretations of a context. Equally revealed is the influence context has on their abilities to advance students' learning.

Ms. Johnson and Ms. Appleyard confessed that they had not thought about many of the issues made public through this study before participating in dialogues with me as a researcher. Yet, dialogues concerning collaboration and the early double planning periods revealed that teachers and administrators often hold varied and incongruent interpretations of a single phenomenon. For example, Mr. Thachery recalled a top-down, principal directed reform, particularly for the first year of reconstitution. He explained:

> I made it plain when I hired them that I was not in the business of trying to win friends. I was brought in to clean up a very bad situation. And so, I wasn't listening to a whole bunch of "whooha." I know that's not a word, but I had a set way that I believed I could get from point A to B. I wasn't interested in, and I know this is going to sound terrible, a lot of what they [the new arrangement of teachers] had to say about how it was going to get done.

According to Mr. Thachery, the initial double planning sessions were directive. The implementation and focus of these sessions were crafted by his hands. He continued to describe a systematic approach in which teachers collected student achievement data from their classrooms based on a prescriptive instructional design:

> I did want teachers to follow the same scope and sequence so that I could review a specific objective to see . . . who had the most consistency in terms of how the students were performing and to look at how that person could serve as a model for the others where there wasn't that level of consistency.

According to Mr. Thachery, he designed the early double planning sessions to focus on student data and teachers' collective engagement in TLIs. Yet, when teachers were asked, "Were the topics for the double planning sessions given to you by the principal or someone outside of your group, or did your group decide the focus of each meeting," unanimous responses revealed that teachers viewed these meetings as being teacher directed and owned. They each explained that the foci of these meetings were generated from within the grade level teams.

These interpretations reveal incongruent (i.e., a critical correspondence) perspectives between teachers and the former principal. What appears to be more accurate is that while teachers may have had control over the "how" of their double planning meeting, administrative forces limited their decisions about the "what." These incongruences, however, may be explained through various postulates, including: 1) a divergence in perceptions; 2) a politics of forgetting; 3) and a romanticizing of one's work.

Divergence in Perceptions

Administrators and teachers, though sharing a particular school space, may genuinely embrace divergent perspectives of a single phenomenon, thereby resulting in a critical correspondence of perceptions. As presented earlier in Chapter Three, teachers and administrators may conceptualize time, particularly teachers' time, in conflicting ways. Their varied perspectives are greater that a polarized debate of who is right or wrong or of philosophical cogitations over whether or not the glass is half full or half empty. An examination of these perspectives is important for understanding the internal movements of school reforms like reconstitution. In the case of Hillside, the juxtaposition of the principal's and teachers' contemplations offers insights into the complexities of leading reform, but more importantly, such juxtaposition may expand the knowledge wealth regarding capacity for teachers' engagement in TLIs.

Smyth (1991) posits that, "There is considerable tension between the way teachers experience schooling and the way policy makers and others perceive that reality" (p. 84). Mr. Thachery (acting as the on-site policy maker who required teachers to meet collaboratively to discuss student achievement data and their TLIs) may have very well perceived the double planning sessions differently from teachers' experienced reality. Conversely, teachers may not understand the theories that guide administrative policy decisions. These divergent perspectives may result from the hierarchical structure of many schools that positions the work of principals and teachers within variant realms of concern. While teachers' work may primarily focus on the needs of students, instructional, and classroom-based concerns, administrators are responsible for coordinating the multiple functions that support teaching and learning at the classroom level (e.g., budget, curriculum, supervision and evaluation, and district accountability demands).

Ms. Lenora alluded to these variant realms of concern during a discussion concerning the uses of classroom-based versus standardized student achievement data. She postulated that while classroom-based and informal assessments might be used to inform teachers' daily classroom instruction, school-wide, standardized assessment data represent "a wakeup call to the principal" and that "there are some things that are not being done by the administration [to ensure that quality TLIs are occurring in all classrooms]." Ms. Adele expressed a comment that also supports the notion of divergent perspectives. She made the claim that working closely with *teachers* provides capacity for engagement in TLIs (emphasis added). For her, other teachers understand "what she is going through in the classroom" whereas administrators and other policy people may have "forgotten what it is like to be in the classroom." That is, teachers share similar realms of concerns, are better able to relate to each other, and are better able to support each other. Ms. Adele extended her explanation:

> You can have all of the administrative support and all this stuff that you want, but they don't know what goes on down at the bottom [in the classroom with children] everyday, day in and day out; So, when you have people who are in the same situation with you, that's your support system.

These findings suggest that, because of their variant realms of concern, classroom teachers and administrators are more likely to hold divergent perspectives of schooling. These variant perspectives may also result from what Hargreaves (1994) defines as a culture of balkanization between teachers and administrators that traditionally places these groups in a dichotomy of "them" versus "us." In this case of Hillside, divergent perspectives between teachers and administrators were real, and these perspectives added to the complexity of the social context of the school—a context that impacts teachers' capacity for engagement in TLIs.

A Politics of Forgetting

Since reconstitution was implemented seven years prior to my initial contact with Hillside, many teachers may not have remembered the fine details of events occurring long ago. Through time and changes in space, teachers come to understand a certain reality of schooling. As they manage the vicissitudes of students' individual academic, social, and emotional needs on a daily basis and as they navigate through the compounding demands of serial reform, teachers may come to define their work according to the immediacy of their context.

Ms. Smith and Mr. Thachery recalled the first years of reconstitution as being a time of immense stress for both the adults and students of Hillside. On this point teachers and the principal were in agreement. The former principal recollected:

> I'm not going to say that the first year wasn't difficult, because it was. We were all getting used to each other [students, faculty, and administration]. Also, we inherited a lot of student behavioral problems. It was about getting the kids acclimated to a level of order.

This recollection is consistent with research that describes newly reconstituted schools as sites of intensified work conditions (Malen et al., 2002; Goldstein et al., 1998). Teachers in these schools often report that learning new curriculums, building new relationships with students, and developing new working relations with fellow teachers and administrators collectively stress their daily work. Such intensification occurring in reconstituted schools often bears down on teachers in ways that eventually define their daily work existence as "surviving the school year." Such intensification may represent a lived experience that traumatizes teachers' memories, leading them into a politics of forgetting. Easley (2003) posits that:

Neither the production of memory nor the act of forgetting is neutral, an apolitical pedagogy. Instead, they offer certain perspectives about what is true. As a pedagogical practice, they operate in ways that define and position a people within a certain social and political realm. This dynamic is designed and enforced through cultural ideology—a political psychology that informs and shapes a collective consciousness of people. (p. 91)

Thus, forgetting the "old" and the "bad" (e.g., the difficult first years of reconstitution or whose directives most likely shaped the content of the double planning sessions) operates as a mechanism for coping with the here and now.

Teachers at Hillside seemed not to dwell in the "what used to be" for the sake of making it through the day and making it through the school year. When dialogues resurrected latent memories, teachers typically replied, "Oh, I had forgotten about that!" They found themselves having to activate their reflective thought system to resurrect dormant memories. The immediate needs of the students, however, seemed to serve as a motivating force for teachers. In fact, Ms. Adele explained that the needs of the students help her to remain focused and committed to students, teaching and learning, and learning innovations on a daily basis. She explained how the needs of students counteract the increased intensification brought on by the endless demands for school reform. The immediate needs of students seemed to keep teachers focused on the present and not the past. Ms. Adele elaborated:

Sometimes you feel like you are just getting beat down, especially with the new rules and regulations [and] when you feel that you are doing everything that you possibly can. [That's when] . . . somebody comes in and puts one more thing on you. You get tired.

She continued:

The needs are what they are, and they are very great. You come to realize after the first year or so, that you can't lose focus. But, meeting the students' needs is what keeps me going. I know I'm not losing focus, because I am here, because I need to be here.

Romanticizing One's Work

Mr. Thachery spoke of recognizing that changes at Hillside would occur by process and over time. He explained that, while teachers initially had little leeway for providing input toward school improvement, their voices were later welcomed. As teachers began to routinely engage in collaboration focused on student achievement data, Mr. Thachery adjusted his leadership role accordingly. Mr. Thachery:

They first needed to demonstrate to me that a level of professional exchange could occur [as exhibited through the double planning sessions]. It got to a

point where they really took ownership of the process. So, my role became
more of one in which I needed to find additional resources for teachers. I
needed to find other opportunities for them to shine . . .

This declaration explains the logic guiding Mr. Thachery's calibrated leadership style. What is presented here is a principal's recognition that, while
change may be ephemerally forced, sustained change results from a leadership
of guidance (Fullan, 2001). Guiding school change entails listening to teachers
and developing leadership throughout the organization. This includes support for
the development of teachers as intellectuals and teachers as leaders.

When asked about the first years of reconstitution, several teachers
responded simply that the first year was difficult. As Ms. Smith recalled, "It was
tough in the beginning." Their recollections of reconstitution were vague, at
best. Yet, their vague responses suggest that perhaps they did not fully understand the theory-of-action guiding reconstitution in the same way as policy
architects or Mr. Thachery. Their recollections were laden with a tone of
distress, reduced to a fleeting memory of a time made difficult by the intensification of reconstitution. In contrast, teachers' memories of the early double
planning sessions carried a more positive tone. Their recollections were stated
with assurance and fervor. What resonated in teachers' minds is a particular
power/knowledge (Foucault, 1979, 1980). This power/knowledge position
recognizes teachers as intellectual meaning makers of their classroom context
and as individuals empowered to make decisions based on their constructed
meanings about contextualized TLIs.

While their memories were incongruent with Mr. Thachery's initial bureau-
cratized double planning sessions, they were congruent with the "leadership as
guidance" style employed by the former principal once teachers became
acclimated to a culture of collaboration. This situation suggests that teachers
may minimize certain memories by romanticizing their work. If so, then, the
teachers at Hillside seem to have purposefully romanticized their work during
the double planning sessions in a way that affirms a particular power/knowledge
position. What surfaces from this practice is teachers' expressed value for
ownership of the double planning sessions (i.e., being able to choose the focus
of these meetings), a high regard for collegial and collaborative decision-making
that is informed by their knowledge of students and students' needs, and an
appreciation for collaborative, professional learning that both derives from and
impacts their "real" classroom experiences.

However, educational researchers and theorists warn that it is important not
to romanticize the "golden years" of education by forgetting the bureaucratic
control and ideological positions around professionalism that have shaped
teachers' work (Robertson, 1996; Hargreaves, 1994). While Mr. Thachery
envisioned collaboration as an opportunity for the analysis of student achievement data in order to inform teachers' collective and individual decisions about

TLIs, Smyth (1991) urges that reflection be taken a step further. He urges that reflection be made critical. As such, critical collaborative reflection unravels and problematizes romanticized ideals of schooling. Symth suggests that reflective collaboration be made critical by:

> creating conditions under which teachers, both individually and collectively, can develop for themselves the capacity to view teaching historically; to treat the contemporary events, practices and structures of teaching problematically (and not to take them for granted); and to examine the surface realities of institutionalized schooling in a search for explanations of its forms and thereby to clarify for themselves alternative courses of educational action that are open to them. (pp. 91-92)

Thus, critical collaborative reflection troubles romanticized vestiges of teachers' historical work context. By problematizing these romantic images, the past comes into focus for the purpose of better understanding one's current work context, the practices, and conditions that shape said context. By critically understanding the context of schools and schooling, teachers are better positioned to "clarify for themselves alternate courses of educational action that are open to them." By critically understanding the contexts of schools and schooling, leaders and policy makers are better positioned to lead school change in ways that are sensitive to the complexities of the context. For teachers at Hillside (and for the purpose of schools to increase and sustain student success), this would mean maximizing their capacity to recognize and engage in the myriad opportunities for TLIs.

Increasing Instructional Capacity through Collaboration

Whether or not Mr. Thachery and the teachers hold fast to incongruent recollections of the initial double planning sessions, teachers were certain of one thing: collaboration occurring during these sessions afforded them the opportunity to expand their instructional repertoires. Expanded repertoires provide the pedagogical capacity for teachers to calibrate their instructional practices in relation to students' learning needs. This was particularly valued for inexperienced teachers joining the Hillside faculty. Ms. Lenora reflected, "Coming in as a young teacher, I had a veteran teacher on my team. And that was helpful." She continued:

> And this teacher had been around for a while. She had seen curriculums come and go and had built up different strategies taken from all of these curriculums over time. She had built up a background knowledge. And so when I had a problem with teaching phonics or how to teach this or how to teach that, she was able to share with me some strategies she had used in the past. For example, she was able to show me how she incorporated some things from "Open

Court" [a previous curriculum] into the word building to help students become more fluent readers.

Collaboration seems to have yielded learning for veteran teachers as well. Such learning results from a genuine exchange of ideas as advanced through collegial relationships among teachers. For instance, Ms. Lenora, though a fledgling at the onset of reconstitution, reported that she and a more experienced teacher developed collaborative ties that enhanced the instructional practices of both partners:

> We really helped each other out. I'm really into the technology and that's my pet project. And she wasn't too much into it. So, she would help me with other aspects in the classroom. And whenever, she needed help with technology, I would help her. So, even though I was a young teacher, she was able to learn from me and I was able to learn from her.

Hargreaves (1994) describes the benefit of collaboration as being multifarious (i.e., providing for moral support and situated certainty, increased efficiency, improved effectiveness, increased capacity for reflection, opportunities to learn, etc.). Ms. Johnson captured multiple benefits of collaboration among teachers:

> This allows us the time to bounce ideas off of one another and to get some strategies that we may not have thought of for handing a specific part of our instruction or a specific part of our classroom management that we are having personal difficulties with. It also gives us ideas from another teacher who is in the same position we are [i.e., working in the classroom with students]. In my case, there are two other teachers on the team.

She concluded that "Three heads are better than one." Conveyed here is a formula for and a potential benefit of collaborative learning—that being collegiality based on trust and candor. For Hillside teachers to divulge their "personal difficulties" within the collaborative, they relied on a certain level of trust among their team members. These collegial and collaborative relationships provided a certain level of support for teachers and break the tradition of isolation that often defines school cultures. These relationships fostered the pedagogical capacity for teachers to better understand their work context, to expand their teaching repertoires, and to engage in TLIs. Ms. Johnson, however, advised that these benefits are best maximized when the double planning sessions are implemented according to its original design that relied on student data and encouraged the ideals of collaboration and collegiality.

Standardization and a Shift in Collaborative Pedagogical Capacity

Since the district's decision to reconstitute Hillside, many conditions account for changes that occurred in the school's context. Teachers and administrators moved on (voluntarily, involuntarily, and/or due to a decline in student enrollment). Comprehensive curricular changes occurred for language arts and mathematics. New district, state, and federal policies were enacted and implemented. Yet, the most striking of these was a shift in reform itself. Reconstitution, at least its onset, represented a grassroots Comprehensive School Reform (CSR). Mr. Thachery was given domain over the selection of new teaching faculty and staff members (along with the assistance of a team of principals, vice principals, instructional supervisors, and other supervisory personnel within the district). He explained, "I had a hiring panel, but I hand picked teachers." Mr. Thachery, by and large, was responsible for the vision, the organizational design that would affect new working relations, and the overall improvement of Hillside (as measured by student achievement scores). Time, however, changed Hillside's context to the extent that the reforms were largely driven by district, state, and national policies. Whether or not the school was still considered to be reconstituted by district standards remained unclear. Clarion, though, was the effect on Ms. Abbey's principalship as a district-driven, standardization of practice was ushered in. Ms. Abbey explained the context of her principalship: "We now have to follow more rigid, district-driven curricular guidelines that focus on basic skills and students' universal proficiency of these skills."

This standardization of practice directly affected teachers' pedagogical capacity to engage in TLIs. Most apparent in the comments of teachers was the districts' and ultimately, Ms. Abbey's laser like curricular focus on reading. They openly shared their concerns for continued professional growth—that is, capacity for engagement in TLIs—commonly recognized as a benefit of the original double planning sessions.

Consistent responses by teachers revealed that while mathematics and reading came to define the stated curricular mantra for Hillside, more district-based emphasis was placed on reading. Two teachers cited the No Child Left Behind Act (and the school's goal to make AYP) as the culprit. Because of the concentrated focus on reading, support for teachers' professional development across the curriculums waned. Ms. Johnson explained:

> To date the professional development that has taken place has focused on communication [reading]. Because of No Child Left Behind, the goal is to get students to a 45% proficiency level [in reading]. And our principal has decided that our main goal is fluency. All of the professional development occurring during our common [double] planning time has been based or geared to communications.

Explicit concerns for professional support were limited to mathematics teachers at the intermediate level (grades three and higher), as teachers at this level either taught mathematics or reading, but not both. These teachers reported feeling left out of an important part of school's professional development programming. Hence, the original design for double planning sessions at the intermediate level was strained due to teachers' varied content areas and the unbalanced support for the reading program. Teachers began to meet for the planning sessions that were organized according to their primary content area. For those who taught reading, these meetings were described as retaining many of the formal elements instituted by Mr. Thachery; those who taught mathematics found themselves left to their own devices regarding the content and structure of their meetings. Ms. Johnson, a mathematics teacher, shared her thoughts:

> So, I've kind of been left out [of the double planning sessions]. I'm not needed there because I'm not teaching communication [reading] this year. So what I do then is end up planning for math on my own, while the other two teachers are involved in the double planning and communications related staff development.

Ms. Lenora, however, was undecided about the purpose behind the unbalanced attention to reading. She elaborated:

> I think to that this year the whole focus in on the reading and the math is sort of to the wayside. Like all of the professional development is geared toward reading. There really isn't an emphasis on math. I'm not sure why. But, it's just not there this year?

What resonated from these perspectives is mathematics teachers' concern about the thin support for their content area. These statements capture a remorse for the loss of a once formally sanctioned practice organized to support teachers' collaborative engagement in TLIs across content areas. These statements also bring into focus teachers' interpretations of reform—interpretations that are informed by their work realities and interpretations that suggest that teachers' primary realm of concern lies at the classroom level and with the goal of instructional efficacy in the particular subject area(s) they teach.

While teachers' realms of concern may vary from those of administrators and policy makers, their concerns are deeply steeped in issues that affect the teaching and learning process. For example, even though Ms. Lenora may not have known the reason behind certain top-down policy decisions nor the principal's narrow curricular attention that placed an emphasis on the school's reading program, she was concerned about how new instructional demands might impact the quality of her teaching. She questioned the extent to which several new policy decisions would prove effective. When asked to provide an example of how the work context had become intensified by the demands of incessant reform, Ms. Lenora explained:

I'm not affected by this so much this year, but the teachers who teach reading are. They are already faced with the emphasis on reading within the 90-minutes block, and now they are going to add a new component. The curriculum was just adopted by the district one or two years ago, and now they are bringing something else in . . . a grammar component. Well, why did you adopt a curriculum that doesn't have everything in the first place? And these things are often done in the middle of the year. Why are you adding new components in the middle of the year? Wait until the summer; have us go to training before school starts. But to start in the middle of the year? Now teachers are forced to learn a curriculum while they are teaching it to the kids. That doesn't make sense.

Her critique implicates policy as a control mechanism that hinders teacher quality to the extent that teachers may find challenge in their ability to adequately teach a new curriculum to their students. Yet, Ms. Lenora's questions do more than problematize the notion of reform intensification as an impediment to the teaching and learning process. Her questions (and those of other teachers) problematize the nature of policy-based reforms as existing only for students—(i.e., new curriculums are added in the middle of the school year in order to advance students' learning while disregarding the learning needs of teachers who are responsible for teaching said curriculums). Sarason (1990) posits that schooling is organized around a disarticulated axiom that "schools do and should exist primarily for students, that is, the aims of education are the aims we have for children" (p. 136). As such, education for children (in this case, school improvement) can very well outweigh its means by serving "an improvement agenda which will in the end only meets instrumental policy interests" (Lodge & Reed, 2003, p. 51). That is, the implementation of reforms to improve student achievement becomes an end in and of itself when minimal regard is paid to the means that support such an aim (e.g., formalized support for teachers' learning of the content to be taught as well as and their capacity to engage in relevant TLIs).

At Hillside, the reform climate seemed focused almost exclusively on a rise in students' academic achievement as measured by the outcomes on a single, high-stakes standardized test. The narrow focus on particular content areas or a certain subgroup of students has been found to be common for low-performing schools that seek primarily to avoid the punishment of policy driven probation (Diamond & Spillane, 2004). For Hillside, this climate was reinforced by district, state, and national agendas to close the achievement gap as well as the ever-present accountability specter lurking in the shadows. Teachers demonstrated how the implementation of reforms to raise test scores in mathematics and reading could ignore the means needed (at least for mathematics) to achieve desired outcomes. For example, because Hillside was a district appointed recipient of federal Reading First funding, teachers of reading regularly met with the principal to discuss student achievement data in this content areas. During an informal conversation, Ms. Jefferson explained that these meetings were required as a provision of the Reading First grant and that they occurred at each grade level. These meetings, to a large extent, were akin to the double planning sessions' initial premise in which teachers collaborated around student data in order to make decisions about TLIs. Yet, teachers of mathematics reported that such support has been nonexistent during the recent school year. Hence, these teachers perceived that content area professional support is an important means for sustaining their capacity to engage in TLIs and for promoting student learning in return. Their assumptions have been corroborated by research that has demonstrated that students learn more during the course of the year when their teachers have participated in content-focused professional development (Harris & Sass, 2007). Their comments suggest that within the teaching and learning process, support for teachers' learning is as important as students' learning. Their comments conveyed a sentiment of loss and displacement within a climate of policy driven reform.

Leading Teachers to Collaborate

The changes in Hillside's context were greatly impacted by leadership decisions occurring from both within and outside of the school. The teachers in this study also identified leadership decisions as having an influence on their capacity to engage in professional development. As stated earlier, Mr. Thachery, the principal, asserted that he set the agenda for many of the double planning sessions during the initial stages of reconstitution, thereby guiding teachers' collective discussions in a particular direction. By all accounts, leadership decisions guiding the design of these planning sessions lead to a practice of collaborative professional development among teachers. These early planning sessions were also monitored administratively through an accountability system that was no longer in place under the leadership of Ms. Abbey. Ms. Lenora:

> We [under the governance of Mr. Thachery] also had to turn in a summary of our double planning. That acted as an accountability measure. Even though you would think that we are professional and should be self-driven, at times there needs to be accountability. We don't have to turn anything in now, so there is no one saying, "What did you do? What did you talk about?" That's part of what's lost.

Because the reform emphasis shifted toward reading, both at the district level and internally under Ms. Abbey's governance, intermediate level teachers of mathematics were not only left to their own devices, no accountability system existed to ensure that they regularly collaborated about teaching and learning. Accountability had been supplanted by an honor system that assumed that mathematics teachers would meet independently to discuss student achievement and TLIs. Yet, Ms. Lenora's reflection raises a critical correspondence regarding the role of accountability in relation to teacher professionalism. Her statement suggests that while conditions that treat teachers as "autonomous intellectuals" (Robertson, 1996) may describe teacher professionalism, such conditions need not be in conflict with accountability measures that hold high expectations for and monitor teachers' engagement in collegial and collaborative decision-making. In fact, accountability measures that ensure collaboration about teaching and learning may spur teachers toward new working conditions—conditions that define a culture of professionalism, collaboration, collegiality, and learning. Deal and Peterson (1999) claim that in order "to have success [in school reform], both new structures and a professional culture are needed." Drawing from a five-year study in two schools serving minority student populations, these researchers report that school success flourished in cultures that focused on "student learning, a commitment to high expectations, social support for innovation, dialogue, and the search for new ideas" (pp. 6-7). Though the context differs from Hillside, such findings bring hope to the notion that a professional culture may develop from an accountability system that holds a high regard for collaboration and innovations in teaching and learning. Furthermore, Ms. Smith's assessment of the early years of reconstitution reminds the reader that, "We [the teachers at Hillside] came together as a team, and that's really what is important." Thus, the accountability driven double planning sessions played a productive role in the development of a culture of collaboration and collegiality.

In the absence of an apparent accountability system and a formal leadership structure that encourages continuous collaboration among intermediate level math teachers, it would appear as though the weekly double planning sessions might have strayed from their original intent. Yet, I observed that teachers in this category continued to meet during the designated double planning time, though liberties were taken to discuss broader educational issues besides mathematics teaching and learning, to include discussions about resources, policies, and the politics of reform. During one session, two teachers began to question the equity of NCLB's student transfer policy. They talked about the backlash of the transfer policy in which the parents of a former student who had been recently expelled from a charter school petitioned for him to be readmitted to Hillside. These teachers speculated that while charter schools can turn students away, schools like Hillside are not afforded the same option. Norguera (2003) explains that for economically disadvantaged families, public schools represent the one social service agency that cannot turn their children away. These comments reveal that teachers in (reconstituted) schools like Hillside have limited control over the context of reform, particularly regarding the population of students assigned to the schools in which they teach as well as other factors that evolve from beyond the walls of their classrooms.

The honor system, in contrast, had sparked an autonomous intellectualism among at least two key-participants as well as other teachers in the school. Ms.

Campbell credited two factors as the primary stimulus for their continued colla-borative ties. These were: (1) a friendship among several teachers of mathemat-ics across intermediate level classrooms (who were not all participants in this study); and (2) a shared concern for the paced curriculum.[3] Ms. Campbell, an intermediate level teacher, told of conversations among her colleagues who collectively shared a concern that the paced curriculum was impeding upon students' ability to do well on the state assessment. She explained that because only a small number of students were able to master skills at a rate tantamount to the curriculum's pace, teachers were finding that many students fell further behind as they advanced to the next grade level. She further expounded on the response that she and other teachers (at the primary level) had taken to retard the possibility that students would perform poorly on the fifth grade, state assess-ment in mathematics:

> A couple of years ago teachers in other classes [at the primary levels] really started asking us to tell them about some of the skills on the [state] test that recur every single year. So we gave them a list. And those teachers work on those concepts as long as they feel that their kids are able to grasp them, even if it is just for mere exposure.

She continued:

> There have been two concepts so far that I have taught to the more advanced class that they remembered from the previous grade. So with that particular class, I didn't have to spend a whole lot of time on those concepts. I think as long as we keep doing that year after year, . . . it will even help us see the gains that we need.

The autonomous intellectualism among these teachers translated into the pedagogical capacity to engage in a TLI that aligns their instructional practices across grade levels in order to ensure the future academic success of students in mathematics. Though narrowly focused around the state assessment, teachers' independent decisions represent a certain level of collective professionalism in which they were able to negotiate their work around the needs of children, thereby creating a small community of practice (Wegner, 1998; Wegner, McDormott & Snyder, 2002) within the broader Hillside teacher populace.

When asked whether or not this community of practice would have devel-oped in the absence of friendship (i.e., trust, candor, and common interests), Ms. Campbell pondered: "I don't know, because I know that a lot of teachers work in complete isolation. We've been in schools where people barely speak to each other and don't work together, so I don't know." She was certain, however, of the goal shared among her colleagues: "But I know for a fact that we are [through commitment and collaboration] going to help out our population of students."

Her statement corroborates earlier findings (see Chapter Three) that place the concerns for students' needs at the center of teachers' contemplations about pedagogical capacity and their engagement in TLIs. Ms. Campbell continued, explaining that conversations among teachers in this group occurred informally during the workday as well as in each other's homes, outside of the school context. This community of practice emerged as a result of informal leadership—leadership that was teacher initiated. For this community of practice, administrative accountability measures were replaced by a collective commitment to serving the needs of students. This commitment drove teachers to create and sustain collegial and collaborative ties for the purpose of raising the achievement level of the students in their classrooms—a feat made possible through a shared TLI.

Discussion

Findings from this chapter reveal that whether manufactured by administrative mandate, known as contrived collegiality (Hargreaves, 1994), or resulting from a search for intimacy among colleagues (Willie & Howey, 1980), collaborative and collegial relationships among teachers (at least in small groups) are common occurrences in schools. Brought into focus are two factors that contribute to teachers' willingness to engage in and to sustain collaborative relationships. These are: (1) a commitment to students (their academic, social, and emotional needs); and (2) the ideal of collaboration that "focuses on the right things" (Fullan, 2001) (i.e., students' learning). Such factors, they believe, will yield the pedagogical capacity for teachers to meet the varied learning and academic support needs of students through the engagement in TLIs. Yet, the goals of leadership influence collaboration within the organization. This is made apparent in the context of Hillside.

This chapter demonstrates that, while teachers' realms of concerns tend to rely heavily on the immediacy of their classroom context, the broader organizational goals, however, may lie elsewhere. The individualized experiences of Hillside's intermediate level mathematics teachers highlight this fact. The district and school level instructional support favored the reading program over other content areas. Thus, district and an institutionalized realm of concern for a particular content area professionally disenfranchised intermediate level mathematics teachers. Moreover, the building principal obediently standardized administrative policies and instructional accountability measures in alignment with the districts' heavy focus on reading. Thus, mathematics teachers were left to their own devices for content specific collaborations and double planning sessions. Autonomy, in this case, provided the necessary capacity for teachers to develop a teacher leadership and self-directed support structures for data-driven collaboration around mathematical teaching and learning. Autonomy also provided the capacity for mathematics teachers to rely on collaborative practices introduced during the tenure of the former principal with little risk of objections from the instated administration. Autonomy, in this regard, reveals that nascent capacity for teachers' engagement in TLIs may not occur through deliberate calculations. Rather, in the case of these mathematics teachers, strict oversight for the reading program diverted Ms. Abbey's authoritative attention elsewhere, opening the door to serendipitous capacity.

This finding demonstrates that teachers, particularly when left alone, may very well develop their own instructional community of practice that influences their engagement in TLIs when particular historical and contemporary conditions provide the relevant pedagogical capacity. In the case of Hillside, teachers had already internalized the foundational commitment to student learning, and were accustomed to collaborative and collegial exchanges that focused on TLIs.

Collaboration within teacher level communities of practice is often informed by teachers' individual classroom experiences, their immediate realms of concern. However, in the absence of a formal network to build coherence among varying realms of concerns throughout the educational system, there is no guarantee that collaboration within teachers' communities of practice will align with building and/or district level goals. Glickman (1993) notes that within school communities, members may express limited thinking that does not include school or district wide concerns. Yet, systemic coherence among members' realms of concerns may provide additional capacity for teachers' engagement in TLIs across content areas and in ways that support school and district wide goals.

Notes

1. Because double planning sessions occurred weekly, much of the student data was classroom based.

2. See Chapter Four.

3. See Chapter Four for a full discussion of teachers' perceptions about the curriculums' pace and their pedagogical capacity for engagement in TLIs.

Chapter Six
Institutionalization of Teaching and Learning Innovations

The teachers of Hillside Elementary School collectively defined teaching and learning innovations (TLIs) as the calibration/differentiation of one's instructional and/or classroom practices according to the diverse learning needs of students. The pedagogical capacity for teachers to engage in TLIs is better understood through an examination of the district culture, which promotes a particular perspective of "differentiated instruction." This institutionalized culture is the direct result of a district lead standardization of practice. For example, teachers attended in-services/staff development workshops focused on differentiated instruction for the teaching of reading. During these in-services (guided by the literacy coach), teachers were reminded of (1) the district's conceptualized importance of differentiated instruction and (2) the district defined components of such instruction. Teachers were reminded that differentiated instruction is important for the urban classroom under federal and state guidelines as recognized for providing an instructional model for meeting the needs of *all* children (emphasis added). Teachers were reminded that the differentiation of instruction "is a teacher's response to the learners' needs" as guided by the following principles: flexible grouping, ongoing assessment and analysis, focused intensity, greater duration, and the alignment of these principles according to students' performance level(s).

The institutionalized emphasis for differentiated instruction was not only reinforced through in-service curriculums but also through policy mandate, as Hillside was a recipient of the federal Reading First (K-3) grant. The school district had recently received a six-year appropriation of $16.2 million, the largest such grant the district had ever received. Hillside was one of 30 Title I schools in the district allotted Reading First monies. As a result, these schools had begun to experience a standardization of practice for teaching as described in Chapter Five. With unwavering control, the district oversaw much of the instructional training, monitored the utilization of prescribed curricular resources and teaching practices, and routinely assessed the outcomes of student learning. The district appointed literacy coaches to each Reading First school. For Hillside, this position was formally known as the Reading Instructional Lead Teacher (ITL) during the early stages of reconstitution. Yet, with the advent of the standardization of the reading programming in these schools, the literacy coaches became the overseers of instruction and the district's liaisons to ensure that teachers implemented the approved curriculum according to design.

During a spring staff development meeting, teachers were informed of a forthcoming federal audit to be conducted by Reading First evaluators. Teachers were asked to maintain thoroughly documented records of systematic student assessment results along with correlating instructional strategies fashioned from these data. The literacy coach, Ms. Brown, announced that the audit would be conducted in schools randomly selected throughout the district during the upcoming academic year. Ms. Brown warned that the audit would be intense, would occur randomly in classrooms (K-3), would include 90 minutes of observations, and the examination of teachers' documented records of students' performance. She added that auditors were also likely to interview teachers about their differentiated instructional practices in relation to on-going student assessment and analysis data.

This chapter seeks to uncover the paradoxes between district defined differentiated instruction and what teachers' identified as TLIs within their classrooms. This chapter simultaneously problematizes the contextual conditions that uniquely define the pedagogical capacity for teachers' engagement in what the district defined as differentiated instruction.

Institutionalized Instructional Practices and Paradoxes of Capacity

When asked to provide an example of what (a) teaching and learning innovation(s) would look like in their classrooms, primary level literacy teachers consistently mentioned the flexible grouping of students (a district defined principle of differentiated instruction). Yet, their descriptions varied with regard to the pedagogical capacity for engagement in this particular form of instructional differentiation. Ms. Smith described both her esteem for and a typical session of flexible grouping that occurs in her classroom:

> We had four/five groups going on. We had one group that was doing word building, building words, writing sentences. We had another group that was doing beginning sounds and letters, building words on the dry erase board, using the dry erase marker with three boxes on it so that they could build short words like "cat" and "hat;" they were also building words, but writing words as well. We had another group doing guided reading, tracking the print, seeing if they could sound out the word as a whole. Then, we had another group using alphabet mats, using a phonemic disk on letters, and seeing if they could guess the sound. And, it was great. There was so much going on at one time, and it really works because you are doing it according to their needs and what these children really, really need. Flexible grouping is a great tool, and I absolutely love it.

Her description identifies the planning and implementation of flexible grouping as the engagement in a TLI because instructional activities were organized according to students' varied skill(s) level(s). In Ms. Smith's classroom, like that of other colleagues who taught at the primary grades, flexible grouping occurred two to three times a week. She explained that in preparation for this

TLI, she creatively pulls together supplemental materials that complement, but extend beyond textbook driven instruction. Thus, for Ms. Smith, flexible grouping also entails the calibration of instructional tools and techniques as informed by a careful read of curricular limits in relation to the learning needs of students.

The influence of the district's mandate for differentiated instruct was not limited to Reading First classrooms, however. In another classroom, students were grouped in pairs as an act of differentiated instruction. Ms. Johnson explained that sometimes students learn best from peer interactions. It has been her experience that students often understand concepts better when clarified by their classroom peers even though she may have previously introduced the same concepts in her own words. Allowing students to dialogue in pairs served as a TLI in Ms. Johnson's classroom. She further explicated:

> We do a lot of partner teaching in here. I have such a gap in ability level. There are some kids who are really strong and others who are really struggling. Quite often the stronger students are willing to work with the lower kids. And, that seems to work very well. So, I try to use peer tutors. A lot of times we will do something in the whole group and then break off to do an activity. The stronger student will sit with the weaker student.

The variant approaches to differentiated instruction (i.e., flexible grouping in Ms. Smith's classroom and "peer tutoring" in Ms. Johnson's room) are representative of the context diversity occurring across classrooms. These divergent methods reflective of the fact that across classrooms, students' needs are different, student dynamics are different, and teachers' responses to students' diverse learning needs are also different, as well as the skills of teachers and their instructional repertoires are variant. Ms. Johnson explained that many students in her classroom were unwilling to struggle with difficult instructional materials and concepts that involve an uncomfortable level of intellectual challenge. She added that when students begin to feel frustrated, they become restless and begin to invite their friends to engage in non-academic activities. Perhaps such intellectual challenges are not developmentally appropriate according to students' functional level(s) or their readiness level(s) to engage in certain instructional assignments, though Ms. Johnson did not apply such level of analysis, at least not during our conversations.

In defense of her decision to place students in pairs for peer tutoring, Ms. Johnson explained that many students possess the potential for completing work independently; yet, their actions expressed a certain level of reticence for independent assignments. Herein lies an example of how the dynamics of students' diverse learning needs (including a collective propensity for a particular learning style) influence teachers' capacity for engagement in a particular TLI. While peer tutoring would appear to offset students' discomfort with independent intellectual struggle, two factors appeared to pose an instructional conundrum that paradoxically challenged both the desired benefit of peer tutoring as well as the likelihood that students in this classroom would value independent learning. The social dynamics and field sensitive learning style (Ramirez, 1991; Claxton & Murrell, 1987; Robinson & Heinen, 1975) of students within her classroom who seek the rewards of social relationships produce an instructional challenge, for Ms. Johnson identified students' persistent desire to engage in non-academic dialogues as a force to be reckoned with—a force that infringes upon the capacity for engagement in the TLI's aimed to promote independent learning as well as to maximize the benefits of peer tutoring. Using one "gifted" student in her classroom as an example, Ms. Johnson explained:

> All the students in here [the classroom] do not need teacher directed instruction. There are some students in here who would be able to take an idea and after showing me that they understood it, they could be off doing things on their own—reading an extra book in that same theme or creating something like a project or researching more information on the internet. I would love to structure my classroom that way. However, even my one student who goes to the gifted program is not an independent learner. I could not say, "You go! This is your assignment for the day. These are the things you need to do." [I could not plan instruction in this way] and expect her to do it. It just wouldn't happen. She would be talking with her friend or bothering somebody, doing something that wasn't academic related. The students dictate my teaching style my classroom.

Hence, while the talkative nature of students may have fueled the communicative ties needed for peer tutoring, peer grouping seemed to serve as a TLI with limited efficacy extent in this particular classroom. Peer tutoring provided the capacity for students to develop informal social skills as well as the infrequent capacity for lower level students to learn from more advances students. Yet, peer tutoring seemed not to support independent learning, nor supply the capacity for the more advanced students to increase their learning through such configurations. Nor did the students' divergent, non-academic conversations exude a passion for the lessons' topics.

As I observed classrooms, it became apparent that this tension yielded a distinct calibration of Ms. Johnson's teaching practices with respect to students' nature to quickly fatigue from independent intellectual struggle. During her mathematics lessons, an alternate mode of instruction resulted, one that was reminiscent of the traditional teacher directed classroom. Whether students were asked to complete hands-on activities or tasks from their text/workbooks, Ms. Johnson guided most of these lessons, keeping students on target and nudging them to think about the lessons' content. In order to gauge students' understanding, she continually posed questions to the whole class and then selected an individual student to respond. Some questions were procedural while others were conceptual. Some questions were surface level while others required reflective cogitations. For example, during a lesson in which the students used drinking straws to create quadrangles, Ms. Johnson posed the following queries to the whole class: "Are they all the same? How many sides do they have? How do you know? What does the prefix 'quad' mean? What if you had a quadrangle in which all of the sides were the same length?"

The above description of Ms. Johnson's instructional response to students' talkative nature offers a particular perspective of teachers' ultimate dependence on their students. According to Metz (1993), teachers ultimately depend upon students for professional satisfaction in such a way that a sense of accomplishment is intricately linked to students' academic performance. For, Ms. Johnson, the academic prowess and social dynamics of the students (i.e., their learning styles, dispositions, attitudes, and skills) were determining factors that guided her teaching/classroom practices. It was apparent that the field-sensitive learning style of students as well as what seemed to be their nature to mistrust their own abilities provided the pedagogical capacity for Ms. Johnson's selected TLI. She explained: "The students [their dispositions and learning styles] dictate my teaching style."

District forces, however, that advocated a standardized practice of instruction in the way of differentiated instruction seemed to exert ill informed mandates that paradoxically compromised the capacity for teachers to make judgments about which instructional practices best meet the needs of the particular students in their classrooms. The district's stanch attention for its particular conceptualization of differentiated instruction resulted from the federal, Reading First guidelines as well as the theory-of-action suggesting that flexible grouping will meet the learning needs of "all" children. Yet, the district's concept of differentiated instruction was narrow and assumed that differentiated instruction is always the best instructional practice, particularly for the teaching of reading, and particularly for urban students. This assumption was revealed through an informal dialogue with a primary level teacher who asked to remain anonymous. This Hillside teacher explained that her classroom population is composed of only lower-level learners and is also an inclusion room for students with special needs. She described her students similarly to those of Ms. Johnson's classroom. She explained the most of the students are not independent learners and are quick to stray off task in the absence of teacher directed instruction. Yet, unlike many inclusion classrooms, a full time para-educator was not assigned to her room. In an earlier dialogue, she too expressed that her instructional decisions are cued by students' dispositions for learning and their learning needs.

Following a school visit, a district representative, however, expressed displeasure with this teacher's instructional delivery and mandated that all of her subsequent reading lessons be taught by placing students in small groups such that each group would concurrently work on specified yet different tasks as a form of differentiated instruction. This teacher was also told not to use workbook nor worksheet activities for small group assignments. These directives were given with little knowledge of the dynamics of this classroom (i.e., the readiness level, learning needs, and dispositions of students, nor the teacher's instructional fortitude for such practice). These directives were given with no suggestions or additional resources to support the mandated instructional changes. These directives were informed by a district-driven standardization of practice advocating small groups as a particular type of differentiated instruction. In response, the teacher took a stance of resistance. She justified her position by exclaiming that she knew the learning styles, dispositions, and needs of her students better than any one time, district observer and that her instructional innovations were planned according to the learning dynamics of her students. She proclaimed that students would not remain on task in small groups without adult assistance—assistance unavailable except when learning support instructors were scheduled to work with students in her classroom. This teacher explained the she would resist the district recommendations until someone from the district could model and demonstrate the effectiveness of said mandates within the context of her classroom and with her students.

Giroux (1983) posits that resistance needs to be viewed from "beyond the immediacy of behavior to the notion of interest that underlies its often hidden logic, a logic that also has to be interpreted through the historical and cultural mediations that shape it" (p. 110). Thus, for this Hillside teacher, resistance is more than a symbol of deviance. Resistance is a critical stance against district mandates upon teachers that are ill informed of the contexts of classrooms. This sort of resistance is a direct challenge to the historically hierarchical governance structure of schooling in which those at the top are empowered to tell teachers what to do because "we know better than you." This example of teacher resistance represents a form of engagement (i.e., thinking about and believing) in a TLI that problematizes a district level, and often hegemonic, disregard for teachers' knowledge of which instructional practices are appropriate for the particular context of their classrooms. Even still, her resistance as engagement in a particular TLI went unchecked by building and district level authorities. Her resistance was neither met by reprimand nor taken up by instructional leaders in any serious manner to evaluate the perceived weaknesses in the districts' rigid definition and application of differentiated instruction.

This teacher was not the only one to find problems with the instructional programming for reading. Ms. Brown explained that the adopted reading program had been designed by local university faculty who often provided training to guide reading coaches' oversight of instructional implementation. It was soon revealed that district-level personnel also found weaknesses in the program. Ms. Brown confessed that she and other reading coaches had reported flaws in the curriculum to the designers during one of their district training sessions. Yet, their assessment, that the program lacked sufficient attention to students' phonemic awareness, was met with a different level of resistance. According to Ms. Brown, university faculty was indifferent to this argument and insisted that coaches direct teachers to deliver the curriculum as written and without deviation.

Research on the schools' adoption of commercial instructional reform models rings a similar tenor. For example, schools that adopt Success for All (SFA) as a model for school reform are often referred to as SFA schools. In many ways, their identity changes, at least publicly. Districts in which large numbers of schools adopt SFA share the same fate. Memphis, Tennessee, and Houston, Texas school districts are examples. Yet, within these districts and schools, teachers and administrators must deal with the daily demands of implementation as they take on the identity of SFA. According to Patricia Gore (Personal Communication, February 1, 2002), director of the National Institute for the Education of at Risk Students,[1] *the model's core is non-negotiable* (emphasis added). Schools must agree to adopt the program as designed by the Success for All Foundation. This means that schools will be provided a SFA facilitator to assist with implementation, but the schools must agree to follow the pre-described curricular and instructional model. They become Success for All schools. However, many teachers cite that the program strips them of instructional flexibility and creativity, thereby causing tension between teachers' beliefs about teaching and the program's design (Borman, Rachuba, Datnow, Alberg, MacIver, Springfield, & Ross, 2000). Lytle (2002) adds that, "In our experiences, developers, are often overly attached to the [reform] models, overly concerned about implementation 'purity,' and not adequately respectful of the need for mutual adaptation in successful program implementation" (p. 166).

While such rigidity is designed to raise student achievement, Lytle (2002) explains that, "effective implementation requires a willingness to approach the hard work of improving urban, minority student achievement as a collective effort" (p. 166). In effect, the change process is often difficult and requires a certain level of finesse. Change is further challenged when reform developers are insensitive to the culture (daily work and struggles) of school-based persons and focus only on implementation purity. In this way, the program runs the risk of becoming an end unto itself. In this way, the program suffers from hyperrationality (Fullan, 2001b) in which vision by itself is insufficient in the face of impatient implementation and the failure of designers to listen to feedback from the field.

The Capacity to Leave No Child Behind
Teachers' capacity to engage in the district defined differentiated instruction (i.e., flexible grouping and concurrent small group instruction) as a TLI was not only dependent upon the learning needs of students. In the context of Hillside's Reading First classrooms, capacity was also dependent upon human capital. Ms. Jefferson clarified:

I feel as though I need another person in the classroom. Since people are limited as to when they can come to help, flexible grouping does not occur often. I feel like I need an extra adult in the room because, at this point, I only have four kids who are truly independent workers and who don't need my assistance to guide them. By having another person to work with the larger group or a small group, we are able to meet the needs of particular groups. So, three or four times a week someone comes in. While they are working with maybe my low group in the morning, they will take the higher group later in the day. I will then work with the lower group. In this way, the needs of the learners are met—doing the same lesson, just at different ability levels.

Thus, for Ms. Jefferson, additional human capital is needed not only to address the diverse skill levels of students in her classroom, but also to accommodate the prominent lack of independent direction and self-determination exhibited by students.

In Ms. Jefferson's reading class, flexible grouping was utilized as a TLI that helps all students to learn the same material, concepts, and information. An emphasis on the calibration of instruction in order that all students might learn the "same thing" is perhaps contextualized by what Ms. Abbey, the principal, referred to as "district-driven curricular guidelines that focus on basic skills and students' universal proficiency of these skills."

These findings reveal that capacity for engagement in TLIs may not only be affected by the learning needs and dispositions of students. Capacity is also affected by an institutionalized regard for implementation purity of program (Reading First) guidelines that emphasize teaching all students the same skills and through a predetermined instructional model (differentiated instruction). Yet, Ms. Jefferson's and other teachers' claims that limited human capital hinders the capacity for engagement in this particular TLI simultaneously critique the notion of leaving no *child* behind at Hillside Elementary.

One commonly expected role of the building level principal is to establish a vision and to set goals that will guide the instructional direction throughout the school. For Ms. Abbey, the No Child Left Behind Act compliments her expectation that every student at Hillside will excel academically. She explained: "I believe in having the expectations that every child can learn and that every child we be instructed to their highest potential is important." She continued: "So I think NCLB regulations gets everyone up to [say], 'Hey, we need to do what we've got to do here, that the [NCLB] goals are good, and the children really can achieve.'"

Even still, Ms. Abbey expressed her personal dissatisfaction with the federal policy. She confessed that NCLB has not provided the additional support previously expected, particularly the resources needed for whole-school reform (across all grade levels). She illustrated:

We have, for example, a [Reading First] grant through the state and federal government that targets K-3 children. My concern is for the fifth grade students who take the state assessment. There is no additional assistance for fifth graders. This summer when we ran the summer program it was with the emphasis of [grades] K-3. If a school had money in their budget, they could pay teachers to work with fifth graders. I didn't have any money, so we didn't do it. So, the fifth graders are getting ready to take the test again in a few months, and they haven't had any real additional assistance. And we have a high population of special needs students here. We are an inclusion school. We're not doing pull-out or separate resource rooms. All of our children are together, [in] mixed ability [classrooms], and we're trying to serve them instructionally where they are [according to their current functional levels(s)]. I guess one concern is for the resources to do this in terms of staff and all.

Ms. Abbey, however, was hopeful that the "new [recently appointed] Secretary of Education for the state is a little more sympathetic to public education . . ." Hence, Ms. Jefferson was not alone in her analysis that additional human capital was needed at the classroom level in order that she might effectively calibrate her instruction for the concomitant flexible grouping of students. At the building level, the principal also identified additional (human and financial) resources as capacity builders for school change and school reform—capacity underdeveloped in relation to her expectations of federal policy. Yet, in the face of such critique there was no mention of a strategic plan for leveraging resources (human or fiscal) in the way of grant writing, innovations in budgeting, or rethinking the school and community relationships.

As I visited classrooms, particular conditions that accounted for the limited human capital available for certain classrooms quickly surfaced. Not only were the financial resources for Reading First restricted to grades K-3, the needed human support identified by Ms. Abbey and Ms. Jefferson began to appear as less of a problem for certain primary classrooms (grades K-2). Much of this support was found in the way of student volunteers and student teachers. As Hillside is located near several major universities, students often volunteer time to assist student in reading. Such assistance was organized through the school's reading center. University tutors regularly pulled students from their classrooms in order to work with them one-on-one. Yet, such volunteerism was not without its challenges. During a fall staff meeting, Ms. Abbey reminded teachers that the university tutors were trained to work with primary students only and with groups of no more than three students at a time. Student teachers too were more frequently placed in primary level classrooms versus intermediate classes. This is particularly true for kindergarten classrooms in which there were multiple student teacher placements throughout the year. In fact, it was not uncommon to see both a student teacher and a student volunteer working concurrently in kindergarten classrooms. The same could not be said for intermediate level classrooms. Rather the inequitable allocation of human capital that emanated both internally (e.g., para-educators and resource teachers) and externally (e.g., volunteers and student teachers) results in an egregious imbalance of capacity for teachers to engage in the district defined TLIs. While such imbalance may be informed by Collins' (2009) cultural and interpersonal domains of power relations (see also Chapter One), it is also contingent upon administrative will that leverages resources on par with the needs of the various units (e.g., primary and intermediate classrooms) within the organization.

Discussion

These teachers' individual and corroborating descriptions of differentiated instruction bring classroom contexts (i.e., the learning needs, dispositions, and learning styles of students as well as human capital) to the forefront as a source of capacity for engagement in TLIs. Capacity within these contexts, however, is simultaneously shaped by conditions outside of the classroom—conditions institutionalized at the school level as mediated by the district according to federal mandate(s) and well as by university practices for pre-service teacher placements. While a particular form of differentiated instruction was an expected instructional method for teaching reading, the institutionalized attention to and encouragement for such a practice had influenced teachers' instructional decisions for mathematics as well. Ms. Johnson's description highlights this fact. Yet, district defined differentiated instruction was applied differently across classrooms and across content areas. For reading, differentiated instruction was specifically conceptualized as flexible grouping. In Ms. Johnson's mathematics classroom, however, differentiated instruction took the form of peer tutoring. During dialogues, other teachers of mathematics also spoke of students working in groups, but their instructional descriptions fell shy of correlating these groups to any type of differentiated instruction akin to that defined by the district.

Capacity for teachers' engagement in TLIs is also contingent upon the availability and coordination of resources. When comparing the distribution of Reading First resources and college student volunteers and student teacher placements according to grade levels within Hillside, a critical question arises. This question problematizes the public's conceptualization of who is a "child." Though Ms. Abbey and federal policy may advocate for leaving no "child" behind, the public's support (financial and human capital) needed to make good on this aim for Hillside was primarily allocated at and limited to the primary grades (K-2) and grade three. Such lack of capacity for older students or the willingness of the public to provide substantial support beyond certain grade levels legitimates the question, "At what elementary grade level does a student cease to be considered a child?" Regarding the missing human capital needed for particular grade level teachers to engage in district defined differentiated instruction as a TLI, this question directly challenges the theoretical, practical, and conceptual interpretations of the title and intent of the No Child Left Behind

Act. This question, particularly for low-income, African American students of Hillside, challenges whether or not the federal government, states, and school districts are willing and/or able to provide the full capacity needed for schools and teachers to address the diverse learning needs of all students. Simultaneously, this question, within the context of Hillside, forces to the surface concern for whether or not future educators are being prepared for or are willing to work with all children or whether they deliberately seek to work with select student populations that represent particular age groups and learning levels and needs. Following this logic, the above question also raises doubt as to whether or not all African American elementary level students at Hillside are considered to be the "children" referenced in the title of the federal NCLB policy. What appears to be more accurate is that younger (particularly kindergarten) learners are regarded as the safe zone while older learners are more likely to be viewed as an undesirable cast—as the young effigies of the Black men and women they are destined to become. These older students no longer appear as children and, therefore, are more likely to be left behind in the pool for capacity building resources (financial and human) that support teachers' engagement in TLIs.

The conditions that limit the fiscal and human capital needed for capacity building in Hillside may be better understood through the convergence of Collin's (2009) cultural, structural, and in some ways interpersonal power domains of institutionalized racism. While emanating from outside the walls of the school, the effects of these racialized power domains are felt deep within the classrooms of Hillside. It would appear that many of the conditions of diminishing resource capacity for the upper grade levels at Hillside mirror many of the broader cultural and structural challenges to school effectiveness.

In the U.S. nine out of ten public school teachers are White and most of them are women. Conversely in 2001, the African American teacher population hovered around 6% (National Education Association, 2003). This is not to disparage the goodwill of this majority White professional population, as many of these teachers enter the classroom with aims of improving the lives of the students with whom they work. Yet, these demographics reflect the cultural domain of power that produces the conditions that tend to steer minority college graduates away from the teaching profession. With the exception of alternate route teachers who, in urban areas, are more likely to be teachers of color and speak a second language other than English (Natriello & Zumwaltz, 2003), the prevailing racial gap among traditionally prepared teachers and their inner-city students makes the limited volunteerism among upper grades in Hillside seem logical, though inequitable.

The cultural and structural power domains converge to define the common characteristics of low-income, urban schools. Of the nation's public school children, it is a known fact that Black and brown children are more likely to attend schools with Black and brown children, and these groups are much more likely that White students to attend high poverty schools (Kober, 2006; Kozol,

2005). And while nearly 30% of new teachers leave education within their first three years and 50% flee within five years, conditions are worse for urban schools serving predominately minority communities. Research has also shown that low-performing, low-income schools with large numbers of minority students are more likely to experience inconsistent staffing from year-to-year in comparison to higher-performing, high-income, and predominately White schools (Johnson, Berg, & Donaldson, 2005). When staffed, the schools of poor children of color are more likely to be employed by inexperienced and under-prepared teachers (Darling-Hammond, 2000). To make matters worse, many of these inexperienced teachers serving low-income minority students are placed in schools that suffer from inequities in funding, resource allocations, and opportunities for students' achievement (Ladson-Billings, 2006; Easley, 2009).

Policy based research that focuses on closing the achievement gap, has begun to investigate the declining achievement of students the longer they remain in the educational system. The Alliance for Excellent Education (2008) explains that "For years, reform and attention has been concentrated on improving the academic outcomes of younger children. . . . But the achievement gains of younger students are not being sustained as they continue through their educational careers" (p. 5). Given these findings regarding the broader educational system, it is no small wonder that given the inequitable allocation of fiscal and human capital at the upper grades, the teachers of Hillside perceive a graduated decline in pedagogical capacity for engagement in TLIs.

Notes

1. The National Institute for the Education of at Risk Students recognizes and provides funding for design and research of comprehensive school reform models that are eligible for school implementation under Title I.

Chapter Seven
The Multidimensionality of Capacity for Teaching and Learning Innovations

Chapters Three through Six have explored and uncovered the connections between teachers' individual and collective contemplations of pedagogical capacity and their engagement in teaching and learning innovations (TLIs). Teachers collectively defined TLIs as the calibration of their instructional and classroom practices in accordance with the diverse learning needs (academic, social, and emotional) of their students. As such, the learning needs of students serve as the cohesion between the variables of pedagogical capacity and teachers' engagement in TLIs.

A macro analysis of these chapters reveals that teachers' practical and day-to-day definition of innovative teaching shatters the notion of innovation as a "cutting-edge," technology based phenomenon. For the teachers of Hillside, teaching and learning innovations are the myriad, ever-changing, and deliberate acts that address the diverse needs of their students. Yet, regarding the connections between teachers' contextualized, individual, and collective contemplations of pedagogical capacity and engagement in TLIs, a prominent concept emerges: pedagogical capacity is immense and is produced through the myriad interrelated elements of schooling. These elements exist throughout the multiple levels and relations that shape the formal process of schooling (e.g., the classroom, building, community, district, state, and national levels). This concept represents a gross analysis of the Hillside context and sheds light on the complex nature of serial comprehensive school reform (CSR), teaching and learning, and the processes of schooling while simultaneously situating the learning needs of students at the core of pedagogical capacity for teachers' engagement in TLIs. What follows is a discussion of the complexities of contextualized pedagogical capacity as revealed through dialogues with teachers and the observation of their work in action. While the examples used here are not exhaustive, they do demonstrate the intricacy of teachers' thoughts about their work context.

The Immense Complexity of Pedagogical Capacity

Chapter One introduced the definition of pedagogical capacity as any and all conditions (e. g., political, social, ideological, and economic) that deny/grant, impede/support, and influence the potential for teachers to engage in formal and informal processes of schooling. Corcoran and Goertz (1995) synthesized the research of others to identify three variables of instructional capacity:

(a) the intellectual ability, knowledge, and skills of teachers and other staff; (b) the quality and quantity of the resources available for teaching, including staffing levels, instructional time, and class size; (c) and the social organization of instruction or instructional culture. (p. 27)

While other variables may be added, this list does highlight the complexity of teachers' instructional capacity that promises to directly influence the teaching and learning process and, as such, more closely reflects classroom level capacity. Chapter Three explored the collective dispositions of teachers as a particular source of pedagogical capacity at the classroom level.

Classroom Level Pedagogical Capacity
Chapter Three revealed that teachers' intrinsic commitment to and their nurturant relationships with students reciprocally provide a particular level of pedagogical capacity for their engagement in TLIs. Teachers' intrinsic commitment to students fuels their will to modify and calibrate their instructional and classroom practices according to the diverse learning needs of students. Supportively, nurturant relationships between teachers and students serve as a mechanism for unveiling the particular needs of students. And, as teachers learn more about their students through nurturant relationships, their commitment to meet the diverse learning needs of students deepens.

Deliberate classroom movements between teachers and their students shape these nurturant relationships. These movements highlight teachers' ethical decisions toward commitment while simultaneously corroborating findings from Chapter Five's discussion regarding the variant realms of concerns between teachers and administrators. While administrators are responsible for coordinating the multiple functions that support teaching and learning at the classroom level (e.g., budget, curriculum, supervision and evaluation, district accountability demands, and policy), teachers' work may primarily focus on the needs of students and instructional and classroom based concerns. Teachers' classroom based realm of concern directly speaks to the notion of location as pedagogy capacity. The classroom provides teachers with an immediate zone of power in which they are able to control their decision-making processes toward instructional and classroom practices. From this level of pedagogical capacity resonates a particular power/knowledge position (Foucault, 1979; 1980). This power/knowledge position recognizes teachers as intellectual meaning makers of their classroom context and as individuals empowered to make decisions based on their constructed meanings about contextualized TLIs.

Local Community as Pedagogy Capacity

Lipman (1998), in her text *Race, Class and Power in School Restructuring*, problematizes each of the issues in the title in a longitudinal, cross-case study of several Chicago high schools. She contends that, "School restructuring has specific meanings in relation to local settings—particular teachers and students, schools, and community" (p. 7). Dialogues with teachers and leaders at Hillside reveal that many of the learning needs of students span beyond purely academic issues. Chapter Five explored the impact of the school's local community as a source of pedagogical capacity. While some teachers identified parents' inability to assist students with homework in mathematics, teachers' collectively perceived a direct relationship between instructional assistance at home and the academic achievement of students. Moreover, several teachers specifically attributed the local community has having an effect on students' social and emotional well-being along with their value of education. For example, Ms. Day and Ms. Appleyard believed that many students come to school from an environment of stress and from difficult family situations. Because of their care and commitment for students, the Hillside teachers collectively made ethical decisions to address the social and emotional needs of their students—needs that are shaped by the community in which the school is located. While their responses were limited to classroom practices, teachers chose to engage in TLIs as a result of the impact that the home/community environment has on students' learning needs. In this way, the community indirectly presents teachers with the pedagogical capacity or, more specifically, a need to modify their classroom practices.

While literature on instructional capacity addresses teacher variables such as their knowledge, skills, and dispositions (Copland, 2003), such research often disregards teacher commitment. Yet, the commitment to students, as demonstrated by teachers at Hillside, troubles familiar race-based findings in other studies of urban (high) schools—findings that present a particular perspective of teachers' beliefs about the conditions of low income, African American students (e.g., Lipman, 1998; Metz, 1993). Lipman's (1998) findings reveal that teachers of class groups different from the low income, African American students in their classrooms, particularly White teachers, are often disconnected from the daily out-of-school lives of their pupils. A pedagogy of place (Haymes, 2003), which defines the category "urban" as a particular type of place with racial meanings, offers (e.g., through media representations and stories by other teachers and students) to culturally and geographically disconnected (White) teachers a certain understanding of African American students and their home environments. As a result, these teachers tend to develop a particular deficiency ideology that is used to describe students as "at risk" for academic failure. Lipman (1998) explains that, in particular, White teachers of non-core academic subject areas were more likely to express a belief that the social conditions of students' home environments created insurmountable obstacles beyond the school's control and beyond their instructional abilities at the classroom level.

The racial composition of Hillside teachers equals that of the key-participants who opened their classrooms and spent time speaking with me—63% White and 37% African American—and reflects a significant contrast to that of the 99.9% African American student body. However, as I observed the Hillside teaching staff, one fact became clear. The relationships between the White teachers and African American students stood in stark contrast to Lipman's findings. More specifically, teachers' interactions with students were racially indistinguishable. For example, all key-participants exhibited an authoritative stance in which they "pushed" and encouraged students to complete assignments (See also Chapter Four). In fact, many of the linguistic expressions used by both African American and White teachers were borrowed from cultural references familiar to students' in an effort to motivate their participation in lessons. These acts demonstrate teachers' commitment and ability to access the cultural capital (different from their own) of their students' lived, out-of-school environments in order to better connect with their students—an example of pedagogical capacity for engagement in TLIs. Furthermore, teachers' expressions of commitment were equally indistinguishable by race.

Building Level Capacity
In the case of Hillside, top-down reform blurred the division between the uniquely building level capacities and those capacities derived from the district's relationship with the school. For example, Chapter Four revealed that while teachers at Hillside had a direct hand in selecting the Harcourt reading program (a decision informed by teachers' understanding of students' collective need to enhance their decoding and phonetic skills), the district-wide adoption and implementation of this series represented a standardization of practice (see also Chapters Five and Six) in which certain instructional demands became standardized by district mandate. Moreover, the state's acceptance of federal Reading First monies, wed both the district and the school to certain federally regulated practices regarding the teaching of reading.

The double planning sessions of Hillside represent a unique example of building level capacity. This example of capacity also highlights the manner in which capacity is context sensitive and may be altered as changes within the context occur. The double planning sessions, in the advent of policy influenced curricular changes, were simultaneously affected by specific leadership responses to the broader political context in which the school existed.

Prior to NCLB, Hillside entered into the CSR implementation process of reconstitution. The local Board of Education's decision to reconstitute the school also limited its control of the school's internal operations, Mr. Thachery, the initial principal, was provided the liberty to lead in a grassroots manner. Thus, he initiated the (grade level) double planning sessions for teachers in hopes that they might develop a collective sense of responsibility for the academic achievement of students. This plan also required teachers to collaborate about their instructional practices and the academic development of students within their grade levels, as informed by a systematic process for tracking and reporting student achievement data. The enactment of NCLB (i.e., Reading First regulations) in many ways usurped the grassroots ideals of reconstitution by ushering in a standardization of practice. As a result, Ms. Abbey's fledgling principalship was deeply influence by a control mechanism that restricted her role as an independent instructional leader, particularly for the language arts programming.

The district's concerted attention to the Reading First programming for schools like Hillside seemed to leverage the principal's unwavering instructional supervision toward implementation purity of the adopted reading curriculum. With this distraction, the leadership and support structures for mathematics shifted. No longer did the school employ a full-time Instructional Lead Teacher (ITL) for mathematics. Rather a district assigned mathematics coach was to divide her time between Hillside and several other schools. Yet, teachers did not make mention of the significance of her visits, nor was her presence made known during my semester-long participation in the school. Teachers of mathematics, for the most part, were left to their own devices in the double planning sessions. In the absence of a formal accountability system to ensure and to monitor their participation in double planning sessions, certain mathematics teachers were provided the capacity to nurture their own leadership skills through what Wegner (1998) and Wegner et al. (2002) call a community practice (i.e., teacher directed double planning sessions). Hence, building level capacity for teachers to collaboratively examine and discuss student learning data for instructional purposes was certainly sensitive to the incessant policy driven reforms occurring within the school.

Hess (1999) contends that the notion of reform has become status quo. He borrows a quote from Chester Finn, former U.S. Assistant Secretary of Education, to question the value of reform as vogue: "'Because of this faddishness, American education often appears to be in the throes of ceaseless change. Yet few of these innovations endure. Fewer yield improved results. And nearly all of them are made within the boundaries of the old design'" (p. 7). The experiences of Hillside teachers reveal that while the wheels of reform continue to turn, there is little guarantee that reform policies will generate adequate building level capacity for teachers to engage in TLIs. This is particularly true in the absence of focused succession planning and strong leadership that seeks to foster coherence among reform initiatives while simultaneously attending to conditions needed to ensure high quality teaching and learning across the curriculums. For example, Chapter Six showed that even when a district-driven standardization of practice resulted in a particular institutionalized definition of TLI, the full capacity needed for teachers to actualize desired instructional methods remained unaccounted for. More specifically, Ms. Johnson cited the dispositions and readiness levels of students as unaccounted for in policy mandates for implementation purity of purchased curriculums while Ms. Jefferson noted the lack of additional human capital needed to actualize the district's plan for differentiated instruction. Because educational reform is typically mired by what Apple (1986) refers to as the "old design" of Tayloristic hierarchy and bureaucracy, schools are often held hostage by top-down policies that are ill informed of the contextually specific variables that influence a schools' potential to fully provide capacity for teachers' engagement in TLIs.

Public Ideology and Policy as Capacity
Beyond the classroom, beyond the school, beyond local communities, and beyond the school district, a broader, public ideology has been constructed to mediate common sense beliefs about student achievement. In Chapter One, the claim was made that standardized test scores have been used as the primary source for measuring achievement of students and the quality of instruction in schools. Such assessments have also been used to identify schools as failing, particularly inner-city, urban schools. Apple (1986) deconstructs the ideology promoted by state sponsored competency tests as such:

> The tests represent and reinforce a redefinition of the content of education as specific skills learning, where skills are defined narrowly. Thus, the language of competency, performance, and effectiveness [as measured by standardized tests] replaces broader language systems centered around knowledge, understanding, and personal development. (p. 147)

Several teachers and the principal, Ms. Abbey, attributed academic success as an opportunity to make a break in one's social status. Yet a read of teachers' discussions about student achievement confirms Apple's position. Within their dialogues, there appeared no language to speak about students' success beyond the confines of a technical rational ideology that attributes academic achievement to a quantifiable, standardized test score. Broader ideological understandings and representations of student achievement shape their small language in this area. The principle behind President Lyndon Johnson's 1965 Elementary and Secondary Educational Act (Title I) was to provide financial assistants to local education agencies (LEAs) serving large populations of low-income families. The goal of such assistance was to raise academic achievement of low-income children to compare favorably with children from other schools. The success of this plan has been and continues to be measured by students' standardized test scores, namely the National Assessment of Education Progress (NAEP). Simply stated, the goal of ESEA historically and contemporarily has been/is to close the achievement gap between low-income students and students from homes of economic privilege—the great Black-White academic gap. As a result of ESEA and texts like *Closing the Educational Achievement Gap: Is Title I Working?* (Kosters and Mast, 2003), not only is educational policy at the nation, state, and local levels shaped by students' academic achievement scores, but the American public (including the teachers of Hillside) has also come to understand student achievement in terms of standardized test scores. Thus, "Good learning is only the accumulation of atomistic skills and facts and answering the questions in standardized achievement tests for students" (Apple, 1986, p. 147).

The debate over the efficacy of standardized testing to advance student learning is by no means moribund nor is it isolated within the walls of Hillside. In fact, the educational advisors for presidential candidates McCain and Obama squared off over this issue during the 2008 primaries. While republican advisor Lisa Graham Keegan contended that standardized testing must be maintained in order to compare student achievement, Linda Darling-Hammond, the democratic advisor, argued that the nation's current standardized tests fail to promote analysis and critical thinking on par with the more high achieving countries on international comparisons.

The Hillside teachers' limited perspectives of students' academic success must be taken with caution, however. At no time did I deliberately prompt them to share their thoughts about broader concepts of student achievement. Yet, teachers' attempts to raise student achievement scores on the state test directly influenced (and provided the pedagogical capacity for) their engagement in TLIs. For example, Chapter Five showed that a small cadre of intermediate level mathematics teachers sought to engage in a TLI that aligned their instructional practices across grade levels in order to ensure students' future readiness to do well on the state test. Even still, these teachers collectively recognized the need to support students' academic success by addressing other issues within the teaching and learning process as well. They recognized students' social, emotional, motivational, and readiness needs as factors to be addressed in order to support students' potential for academic achievement. Such recognition symbolizes teachers' commitment to the children they serve as well as their understanding that the pedagogical capacity for engagement in TLIs is simultaneously and always affected by variables far beyond the classroom, beyond the school, beyond the design of policy, and beyond the public's limited conceptualization of student achievement.

The Audacity to Teach

These examples demonstrate the complexity of pedagogical capacity for teachers' audacity to engage in TLIs in Hillside Elementary School. As demonstrated here, pedagogical capacity is complex, not simply because it emanates from multiple stations and elements (e.g., classroom level, school level, community level) within the process of schooling, but because these are relational, interrelated, and exist as gears within larger social, political, and educational systems. Furthermore, such complexity troubles the notion of capacity as the "potential of material, a product, person, or group to fulfill a function if it is used in a particular [intended and deliberate] way" (Newmann et al., 2001, p. 261). For example, Chapter Six captured the duality of capacity by examining an institutionalized TLI (differentiated instruction). Hillside's concept of differentiated instruction resulted from a district defined instructional policy and practice, as influenced by NCLB's Reading First regulations.

As a result of a district defined, institutionalized TLI, teachers were instructed to follow the principles of flexible grouping, ongoing assessment and analysis, focused intensity, greater duration, and alignment of these principles according to students' performance level(s). Conversations with teachers who explicitly named differentiated instruction as a consideration of their instructional repertoire revealed their unique classroom-based interpretations and application of this institutionalized TLI. These teachers collectively defined differentiated instruction as a practice of placing student into groups; yet, they also identified certain "zones of wishful thinking" (Hill & Celio, 1998) embedded within the district's design for this instructional method. While district expectations may have provided the capacity for teachers to place students into groups according to teachers' discretion and regarding students' ability levels, teachers also identified the learning and social dispositions of students as well as human capital as impeding their capacity. These zones of wishful thinking result in the duality of pedagogical capacity that may be produced by a single policy mandate.

Recalling specific examples, the experience of an anonymous teacher revealed that a district representative's suggestion that she engage in differentiated instruction (that she conduct all reading instruction utilizing a configuration of concurrent small groups) emerged from a district mandate—a mandate ignorant of the contextualized student characteristics of this teacher's particular classroom. Furthermore, Ms. Jefferson explained that her engagement in differentiated instruction is contingent upon additional human capital that is needed not only to address the diverse skill levels of students in her classrooms, but also to accommodate the prominent lack of independent direction and self-guidance exhibited by students. Hence, the district-driven mandate for differentiated instruction, as interpreted by teachers, assumes that placing students in independently governed small groups will provide teachers with the capacity to address the learning needs of "all" students. Yet, teachers' experiences with such an instructional practice leads the reader to believe that such differentiated instruction has limited use in the absence of students' readiness or skills for independent, self-directed learning or in the absence of additional adults to help monitor the multiple, concurrent small group sessions. The district's lack of such knowledge places the mandate for differentiated instruction within a zone of wishful thinking while simultaneously forcing to the surface the duality of pedagogical capacity.

While the pedagogical capacity for teachers' engagement in TLIs may result from the amalgamated relations between multiple levels of decision-making and actions, the classroom remains the primary location of the core technology of schools. Dialogues with and observations of teachers reveal that they perceived that their engagement in TLIs serves to meet the learning needs of students. Yet, they also perceived the need for pedagogical capacity in order to maximize the potential of their engagement. This finding places pedagogical capacity at the nexus of teaching and learning. And while factors like a principal's clearly articulated school mission and vision, collaboration among peers, and parental support may provide a certain level of pedagogical capacity, this study revealed that classroom level capacity most directly influences teachers' engagement in teaching and learning innovations.

Teachers have identified numerous factors as promoting classroom level pedagogical capacity. Three prominent examples are teachers' nurturant relationships with students, their commitment to the students they serve, and the use of informal, classroom assessment practices. Each is undergirded by teachers' ethical and intellectual decision-making. These decisions refer to teachers' intrinsic and moral desire to make a difference in the lives of the students they teach. These decisions are also shaped by their interpretations of policy demands, resource allotments, and other contextualized variables within their workplace. Moreover, their interpretations represent teachers' (classroom level) realm of concern as well as their value for the immediate pedagogical capacity needed to address the vicissitudes of students' varied learning needs.

While pedagogical capacity in general is complex (existing with a multi-layered educational system that produces both favorable and negative results), classroom level capacity for TLIs is equally multifarious and may be understood as the least common denominator for teachers' ability to address the diverse learning needs, that is, the actualization of their audacity to engage in TLIs. Figure C. highlights the gross analysis of such complexities as revealed through my work with the teachers of Hillside. Teachers' contemplations of pedagogical capacity and engagement in TLIs are centrally focused at the classroom level and are coupled by the diverse learning needs of students. Teachers' intrinsic, ethical decisions and their interpretations of broader contextualized variables are influenced by students' needs as well as the systemic pedagogical capacity for and their engagement in TLIs.[1] While all variables affecting these relationships are not specifically named, they are recognized in the broader concepts of district policy, state policy, national policy, and the local community.[2] These relationships and contemplations are important for informing the profession about the complexities of the pedagogical capacity for those with the audacity to teach.

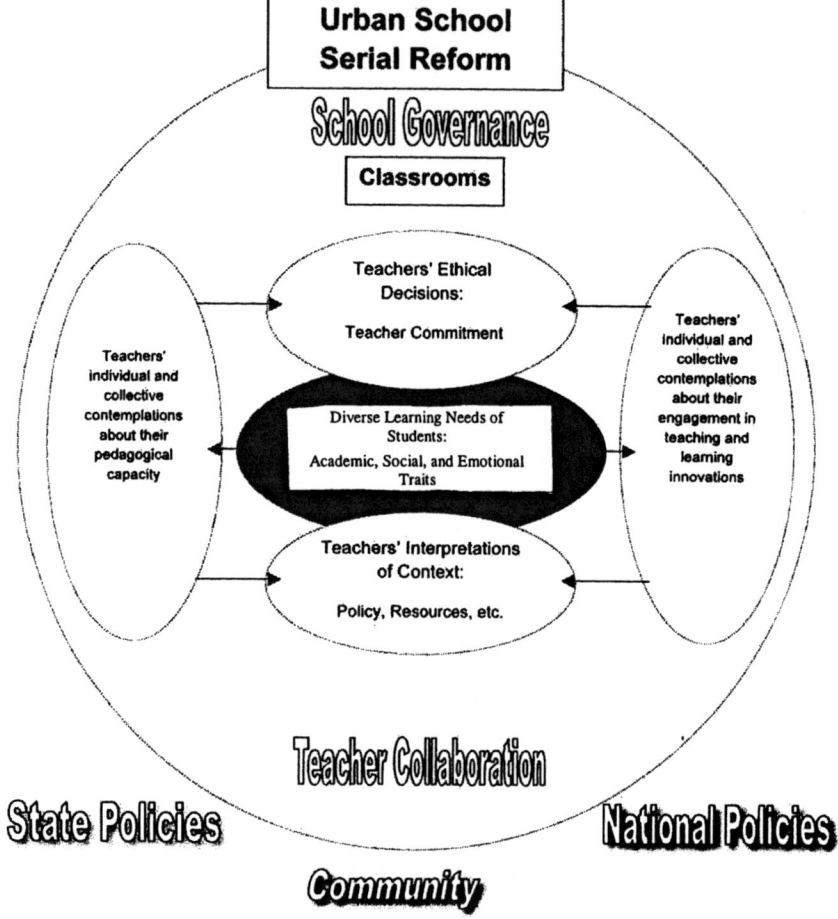

Figure C. The Complex Connections between Pedagogical Capacity and Teachers' Engagement in Teaching and Learning Innovations

Implications for Systemic Pedagogical Capacity

A gross analysis of the aforementioned chapters, observational data, and dialogues with teachers during their daily routines confirm that the complexity of school reform is real and that such complexity has a real effect on the pedagogical capacity for teachers' engagement in TLIs at the classroom level.

Simply, the complexities of school reform intensify teachers' work. As an illustration of such intensified work space, introduced here is a teacher's commentary not previously mentioned. Ms. Adele explained:

> The school-based rules are fine . . . but it's the outside influences. The outside agencies [NCLB and the district] keep saying, "You have to do this. You have to do that." Sometimes you feel like, if they come in that door with one more piece of paper, you are just going to leave. Like I said, it's not the children, it's not the curriculum. It is none of that. It's the constant changing [of] things, instead of letting things that work. I mean . . . [education is] influenced too much by people who are not educators?

Her comment captures a teacher's perspective of classroom intensification as brought on by serial, top-down policy mandates and other externally initiated demands. Ms. Adele was not alone, however; other teachers, as previously discussed, also shared this sentiment of intensification as brought on by factors beyond the classroom and beyond teachers' control.

This point is made here in order to underscore several important implications gleaned from Hillside regarding the bureaucratic design of schooling and serial reform implementation in relation to the connections between teachers' perceived pedagogical capacity and their engagement in TLIs. While several of these issues were briefly introduced earlier, they, along with others, are further developed here. They reflect a systems approach for educational excellence. These are: (1) the downturn of a pedagogy of blame; (2) the language of achievement, (3) and the acknowledgement of a pedagogy of diversion. Each represents implications for a reconceptualization of certain practices and ideologies that currently inform school reform, urban schooling, and the pedagogical capacity for teachers' engagement in TLIs.

The Downturn of a Pedagogy of Blame
A review of literature related to Hillside revealed that education is an inherently political system (Jones & Malen, 2002; Easley, 2005). As such, various perspectives of blame can be found to explain the alleged failures in education. Districts blame schools, America blames its teachers, and teachers blame parents. Such action can be understood as a pedagogy of blame, which legitimates actions similar to a game of dodge ball or a system of unidirectional accountability. For example, reconstituted schools are often promised additional resources that were not provided prior to district decree for restructuring its school(s) (Malen et al., 2002; Goldstein et al., 1998). As such, the prior teachers and administrators were expected to work in conditions of limited resources under the watchful eye of the district. Acting through a "theory of remedy" (Goldstein et al., 1998), the district essentially blames the schools' former employees for failure while |excusing itself of fault, as it promises change and future building level success to the public.

In the case of Hillside, reconstitution did not lead to the materialization or the sustainability for the full range of resources promised. For example, the technology theme was not thoroughly supported with the needed infrastructure for school-wide, state of the art technologically rich instruction. Nor was the school provided onsite maintenance for the upkeep of machinery. Similarly, the implementation of NCLB did not result in the expected resources. Many critics of the policy like the National Education Association (2003) have made the claim that the policy forces upon states new, underfunded mandates, which it says violates a provision of NCLB. Ms. Abbey's assessment of this situation reminds the reader of the ways in which NCLB unexpectedly and financially impacted building level capacity:

> It hasn't turned out to be additional resources for us [as related to the NCLB resource allotment for Hillside Elementary School]. The faculty has taken on the mission to leave no child behind. It's just that when I'm saying we need all children proficient, teachers are looking at me saying, "OK, we have the curriculum; we are here every day, but we need some assistance in terms of having smaller class size, in terms of having after school programs that are of quality and that really connect with our work and other programs." We're just getting small measures of that.

Cases of inadequate or ephemeral financial allocations from the top down are not uncommon. A comparative literature review of the federally recognized comprehensive school reform models Success For All, The Edison Project, and reconstitution revealed that schools entering into these models are initially promised additional financial, human, and/or technological support. Yet, support is often decreased as improvement occurs. The belief here is that once positive change has been produce, schools will be able sustain such change through their own devices (Goldstein et al, 1998). In reality, as new teachers join schools and change begets new challenges to reckon with, support should not be decreased but increased. From an administrative perspective, Lytle (2002) further explains:

> consultant support [from external reform designers and district officials] should be increased, not decreased, as schools move into the third and fourth years of implementation. As the [reform] models evolve and school staffing changes, the need for related professional development continues. School budgets need to reflect these costs. (p. 166)

In fact, the 1990's RAND research on New American Schools' reform models showed that the lack of funding was the single most important reason why most schools decided to drop a previously adopted reform design (Berends et al., 2002).

In the absence of reciprocal accountability (Goldstein et al., 1998; Easley, 2005), policy architects and top-level policy administrators are able to privately and discreetly renege on their promises to provide schools with additional resources (Malen et. al, 2002). Within the current hierarchical design of education, those at the top retain the legitimate power to publicly blame schools for their inability to sustain improvements, even when the money is gone. In the absence of reciprocal accountability, a pedagogy of blame often works most effectively (though not definitively speaking) from a position of power and in a top-down direction. Hillside has experienced a standardization of practice as a result of NCLB and district mandates. These mandates implicate the school and teachers for students' low achievement while simultaneously suggesting that those at the top know what's best for schools, teachers, and students within the political game of dodging the blame. What is needed, however, is a reciprocal accountability relationship in which all stakeholders are responsible for the intellectual growth of students and the success of schooling as an institution. Within such a relationship, those furthest away from the classroom and furthest away from the lowest rung of the current educational system are equally implicated in the failure of schools to leave no child behind, particularly when the legitimate need for resources and support have been identified but not provided.

The Language of Achievement
Much of the dialogue among Hillside's teachers on the topic of student achievement has been couched in limited terms. Historically and contemporarily, academic achievement in/for American schools has been defined through an epistemology of comparison that requires quantifiable measures, that is, a practice of standardization—standardized curriculums, standardized test scores, and a standardized conceptualization of educational effectiveness. This language, over time, has come to be publicly accepted as common sense and rational and has been mediated through/by media representations, policy, and research on academic achievement. A look at Hillside Elementary School has revealed that such common sense thinking also governs teachers' talk and work around student achievement.

Though the teachers at Hillside recognized and deliberately calibrated their instructional and classroom practices in relation to the broader learning needs of students (i.e., social and emotional traits as well as motivational needs that may be shaped by students day-to-day, out-of-school lived experiences), their language of achievement was limited by a commonly accepted and hegemonic understanding that a standardized test score is "the measure" of students' success. Nor did their efforts to address these broader learning needs appear to be valued by district leaders or instructional facilitators. In reality, high-stakes accountability reforms often focus on an immediate increase in student achievement, as measured by test scores. As such, those players furthest away from the classroom tend to be least concerned with the specific and diverse learning needs of students, as recognized by classroom teachers. Their top-down decisions tend not to reflect an interest for the day-to-day, contextualized calibrations and differentiations that teachers engage in at the classroom level, as informed by the learning needs of students. However, their expectations for classroom and building level outcomes on standardized achievement measures shape the conditions that lead teachers to purposefully prioritize their instruction according to those practices that are rewarded (Robertson, 1996). These expectations simultaneously shape teachers' language around student achievement.

Yet, a high standard for student achievement and a standardization of achievement are not necessarily equivalent. Whereas a high standard for student achievement may easily accommodate the varied learning needs of students by recognizing the academic growth of students individually, a standardization of achievement may not. For example, NCLB requires that students collectively and quantifiably produce a certain level of achievement each year. This process is known as meeting adequate yearly progress (AYP). It is unlikely that such a mandate will fade in the near future for the fear among political figureheads that they may be viewed as lowering the standards for student achievement. In the case of Hillside, test scores from each year's fifth grade cohort are compared, quantifiably, in order to determine AYP. Such is the standardization of achievement—a comparison of one cohort of students to another in order to measure a standardized achievement—that down plays the individual success of students, no matter how small in comparison to others. Ms. Jefferson's explanation reminds the reader:

> [through informal assessments,] I can see that the children have progressed, even if it is by one or two percent, which may seem small to the state and others who collect the data, but that is huge for many of our kids. So, [because of the significance these small gains for some children] that means more to me than the 10 percent the state would ask for.

Conversely, a high standard for student achievement acts in response to what Ms. Jefferson and the other teachers at Hillside have identified as the diverse learning needs of students in which several teachers expressed needed to be honored by recognizing the gains of all students, regardless of how small or large. As such, the measure of achievement rests in a comparison of growth for the individual learner from the beginning to the end of an academic school year. In this manner, each student is judged by his or her own merit, is supported according to his or her unique learning needs, and is honored for his or her individual talents. The aim, then, is to ensure that each student reaches his or her maximum potential. In this manner the common sense understanding of student achievement is supplanted by the broader notion of student success.

The Acknowledgement of a Pedagogy of Diversion
The limited scope of achievement presented here, acts as a "pedagogy of diversion" (Giroux, 1997) that is concomitantly played out at multiple levels. Noguera (Personal Communication, April 14, 2004) contends that top-down

policy/decision makers often ignore the conditions in which urban teachers have to work. This means that they not only ignore the physical conditions and li-mited resources of many buildings, as described by Anyon (1997) and Kozol (1991)—conditions that deter teachers' willingness to remain in the profes-sion—but also the community based conditions that affect the learning needs of students. In such cases, top-down mandates assume that a one size instructional and curricular treatment will serve the learning needs of *all* students, particularly for low performing, inner city, urban schools thought to be in need of fixing. This assumption ignores the diverse learning needs of students as well as the varied levels of capacity needed for teachers to individually and collectively address the needs of students in their classrooms. At the classroom level, a standardization of practice may result in a pedagogical diversion that teaches students the basic skills needed to pass the test—one of the codes of academic achievement—while simultaneously leaving them inept of the cultural, social, emotional, and intellectual capitals needed to broach the broader sociopolitical and economic systems that exist beyond their immediate neighborhoods.

To understand these pedagogical diversions is to question the extent to which the current educational system provides a "good" education to certain student populations. As deeply steeped in the current educational system, these pedagogical diversions also do little to advance the ideal "that a good education is an essential foundation for success in terms of the material, social and civic aspects of American life" (Hirschland & Steinmo, 2003, p. 334). They fail to support students' development of the intellectual and emotional capacities needed to mediate their personal lives and the conditions in which they live. To understand these pedagogical diversions is to question the historical and contemporary language of achievement for all students.

However, reform decisions that result from dialogues and public delibera-tions with schools (regarding pedagogical capacity for teachers' engagement in TLIs) and families serve as a more accurate method for meeting and addressing the diverse learning needs of students. While such a tactic may seem unusual and radical within a commonsense logic of a top-down educational system, particularly for reforms enacted at the national level, such acts are needed in order to sponsor the full development and academic success of students. Such acts are useful for uncovering and nurturing the intellectual and emotional capacities students need to mediate their personal lives, which in turn influence their academic growth. Such acts require that policies are made in counsel with schools and parents and that programs are designed collaboratively with the input of schools and parents. This also means that agendas for healthy school-family relationships are set collaboratively and not by schools for families, in the absence of understanding their needs, values, motivations, and capacities to support students' academic development.

Taken together, the reconceptualiztion of the current unidirectional pedagogy of blame, an expanded notion of student success, the examination of institutionalized pedagogies of diversion, along with understanding the function of capacity for teachers' engagement in teaching and learning innovations, these do not represent a new school reform in and of themselves. Rather, they more accurately reflect an entrée into a bold, new order of schooling, one that troubles traditional norms and ideologies and is organized around systems of coherence—systems that work in tandem, continually balancing one another, simultaneously from the top-down and bottom-up. This new order, however, requires the commitment among policy makers, educators, and even the public to support those with the audacity to teach for the individual and collective successes of American students.

Notes

1. While the arrows in Figure C. are one directional, they are not static and are representative of this study's gross analysis of the relationships between teachers' individual and collective contemplations of pedagogical capacity and their engagement in teaching and learning innovations.

2. Examples of these variables include reconstitution, NCLB, a district driven standardization of practice, and institutionalized teaching and learning innovation, statewide (standardized) assessment, and parents' instructional support for homework.

References

Adelman, C. (1989). The practical ethic takes priority over methodology. In. W. Carr (Ed.), *Quality in teaching: Arguments for a reflective profession* (pp. 173-182). New York: Falmer Press.

Al-Hawamdeh, S. (2002). Knowledge management: Re-thinking information management and facing the challenges of managing tacit knowledge. *Information Research,* 8 (1), paper No. 143 [Available at http://InformationR.net/ir/8-1/paper143.html].

Alliance for Excellent Education (2008). *From no child left behind to every child a graduate.* Washington, DC: Author.

Anyon, J. (1997). *Ghetto schooling: A political economy of urban educational reform.* New York: Teachers College Press.

Apple, M. W. (1982). *Education and power.* Boston: Routledge & Kegan Paul.

———. (1986). *Teachers and texts: A political economy of class and gender relations in education.* New York: Routledge & Kegan Paul.

———. (1996). *Cultural politics and education.* New York: Teachers College Press.

Argyris, C. & Schön, D. A. (1974). *Theory in practice: Increasing professional effectiveness.* San Francisco: Jossey-Bass.

Ascher, C. (1988). Improving the school-home connection for low-income urban parents. (ERIC Document Reproduction Service No. ED 293 973).

Ayers, W. (1995). *To become a teacher: Making a difference children's lives.* New York: Teachers College Press.

Bailey, L. B. (2002). *Training teachers to design constructivist reading homework.* Dissertation Abstract International, 63(078) 2507.

Berends, M., Bodilly, S. & Kirby, S. N. (2002). Looking back over a decade of whole-school reform: The experience of New American Schools. *Phi Delta Kappan,* 84(2), 168-175.

Borman, G. D., Rachuba, L., Datnow, A., Alberg, M., MacIver, M. M., Stringfield, S., & Ross, S. (2000). Four Models of School Improvement. *Successes and challenges in reforming low-performing, high poverty title I schools* (Tech. Rep. No. 48). Johns Hopkins University & University of Memphis, Center for Research on the Education of Students Placed at Risk.

Brown, J. S., & Duguid, P. (2000). *The social life of information.* Boston: Harvard Business School Press.

Bryan, J., & Burstein, K. & Bryan, T. (2001). Students with learning disabilities: Homework problems and promising practices. *Educational Psychologist, 36*(3), 167-180.

Bushnell, M. (2003). Teachers in the schoolhouse panopticon: Complicity and resistance. *Education and Urban Society,* 35(3), 251-272.

Clark, C. & Peterson, P. L. (1986). Teachers' thought processes. In M. C. Wittrock (Ed.), *Handbook of Research on Teaching* (3rd ed., pp 255-296). New York: Macmillan.

Claxton, C. S., & Murrell, P. H. (1987). Learning styles: Implications for improving educational practices. *ASHE-EPIC Higher Education Report* No. 4. Washington, DC: Association for the Study of Higher Education.

Cohen, D. K., Raudenbush, S. W., & Ball, D. L. (2003). Resources, instruction, and research. *Educational Evaluation and Policy Analysis,* 25(2), 119-142.

Collins, P. H. (2009). *Another kind of public education: Race, schools, the media, and democratic possibilities.* Boston, MA: Beacon Press.

Comer, J. P. & Haynes, N. M. (1991). Parental involvement in schools: An ecological approach. *Elementary School Journal,* 91(3), 271-177.

Conant, J. B. (1961). *Slums & suburbs: A commentary on schools in metropolitan areas.* New York: McGraw-Hill.

Cooper, R. & Jordan, W. J. (2003). Cultural issues in comprehensive school reform. *Urban Education,* 38(4), 380-397.

Copland, M.A. (2003). Leadership of inquiry: Building and sustaining capacity for school improvement. *Educational Evaluation and Policy Analysis,* 25(4), 375-395.

Corcoran, T. & Goertz, M. (1995). Instructional capacity and high performance schools. *Educational Researcher,* 24 (9), 27-31.

Dahl, K. L., Scharer, P. L., Lawson, L. L., & Grogan, P. R. (1999). Phonics instruction and student achievement in whole language first grade classrooms. *Reading Research Quarterly,* 34(3), 312-341.

Danielewicz, J. (2001). *Teaching selves: Identity, pedagogy and teacher education.* New York: State University of New York Press.

Darling-Hammond, L. (2000). Teacher quality and student achievement: A review of state policy evidence. *Educational Policy Analysis Archives,* 8(1).

Darling-Hammond, L. (Ed.) (2005). *Professional development schools: Schools for developing a profession* (2nd ed.). New York: Teachers College Press.

Darling-Hammond, L. (2007). The flat earth and education: How America's commitment to equity will determine our future. *Educational Researcher,* 36(6), 318-334.

Deal, T. E. & Peterson, K. D. (1999). *Shaping school culture: The heart of leadership.* San Francisco: Jossey-Bass.

Delpit, L. (1995). *Other people's children: Cultural conflict in the classroom.* New York: The New Press.

Desimone, L. M., Porter, A. C., Garet, M. S., Yoon, K. S., Birman, B. F. (Summer, 2002). Effects of professional development on teachers' instruction: Results from a three-year longitudinal study. *Educational Evaluation and Policy Analysis,* 24(2), 81-112.

Diamond, J. & Spillane, J. (2004). High-stakes accountability in urban elementary schools: Challenging or reproducing inequality? *Teachers College Record,* 106(6), 1145-1176.

DuFour, R. (2004). Schools as learning communities. *Educational Leadership,* 61(8), 6-11.

DuFour, R. & Eaker, R. (1998). *Professional learning communities at work: Best practices for enhancing student achievement.* Bloomington, IA: National Education Service.

Easley, J. II. (2003). Who let the dogz out!: Media ,memory, the market, and the evolution of urban black maleness. In L. A. Allen, D. A. Breault, D. Cartner, C. Chargois, R. Gaztambide-Fernandez, M. Hayes, K. Krasny, & B. Setser, (Eds.), *Curriculum and pedagogy for peace and sustainability* (pp. 87-99). NY: Educator's International Press.

———. (2005). The political tension of education as a public good: The voice of a Martin Luther King Jr. Scholar. *Urban Education and Society,* 37(4), 1-16.

———. (2006). Alternative route urban teacher retention and implications for principals' moral leadership. *Educational Studies,* 32(3), 241-249.

———. (2009). What do students know anyway?: High school graduates' perceptions of standards and implications for educational improvement. *Journal of Urban Learning, Teaching and Research, 5,* 15-20.

Easley, J. II, Henning, M. B., & Bradley, B. (2003). Finding graduate student voices through the deconstruction of democratic relationships in a PDS. *The Professional Educator, 25*(2), 55-65.

Education Week/Pew Charitable Trust (1988). *Quality counts '98: The urban challenge-public education in the 50 states* (Vol. XVII, No. 17). Washington, DC: Author.

Elmore, R. F. (1979). Backward mapping: Implementation research and policy decisions. *Political Science Quarterly, 94*(4), 601-616.

English, F. W. & Steffy, B. E. (2001). *Deep curriculum alignment: Creating a level playing field for all children on high-stakes tests of educational accountability.* Lanham, MD: Scarecrow Press.

Finn, C. E., Jr. (1992). Introduction. In C. E. Finn, Jr. & T. Rebarber (Eds.), *Education Reform in the '90s.* New York: MacMillan.

Firestone, W. A. & Pennell, J. R. (1993). Teacher commitment, working conditions, and differential incentive policies. *Review of Educational Research, 63*(4), 498-525.

Foucault, M. (1979). *Discipline and punish: The birth of the prison* (A. Sheridan, Trans.). New York: Vintage Books.

———. (1980). *Power/Knowledge.* Brighton: Harvester.

Fullan, M. (2001). *Leading in a culture of change.* San Francisco: Jossey-Bass.

———. (2001b). *The new meaning of educational change.* (3rd. Ed.). New York: Teachers College Press.

Friere, P. (1970). Pedagogy of the oppressed. New York: Continuum.

Gillian, C. (1982). *In a different voice.* Cambridge, MA: Harvard University Press.

Giroux, H. A. (1981). *Ideology, culture, and the process of schooling.* Philadelphia: Temple Press.

———. (1997). Rewriting the discourse of racial identity: Towards a pedagogy and politics of whiteness. *Harvard Education Review, 67*(2), 285-320.

———. (1983). *Theory & resistance in education: A pedagogy for the opposition.* New York: Bergin & Garvey.

———. (1988). *Teachers as intellectuals: Toward a critical pedagogy of learning.* New York: Bergin & Garvey.

Giroux, H. A., & Simon, R. I. (1989). Schooling, popular culture, and a pedagogy of possibility. In H. Giroux & R. Simon (Eds.), *Popular culture, schooling and everyday life* (pp. 219-235). Wesport, CT: Bergin and Garvey Press.

Glickman, C. D. (1993). *Renewing America's schools: A guide for school-based action.* San Francisco: Jossey-Bass.

Goldstein, J., Kelemen, M., & Koski, W. (1998). *Reconstitution in theory and practice: The experience of San Francisco.* Paper Presented at the Annual Meeting of the American Educational Research Association, San Diego, CA. April 13-17, 1998.

Goodlad, J. I. (1984). *A place called school: Prospects for the future.* New York: McGraw-Hill.

Griffin, G. A (1987). The school in society and social organization of the school: Implications for staff development. In M. F. Wideen & I. Andrews (Eds.), *Staff development for school improvement: A focus on the teacher.* New York: The Falmer Press.

Hargreaves, A. (1994). *Changing teachers, changing times: Teachers' work and culture in the postmodern age.* New York: Teachers College Press.

Harris, D. N., & Herrington, C. D. (2006). Accountability, standards, and the growing achievement gap: Lessons from the past half-century. *American Journal of Education*, 112(2), 209-238.

Harris, D. N., & Sass, T. (2007). *Teacher training, teacher quality and student achievement* (CALDER Working Paper 3).

Haymes, S. N. (2003). Toward a pedagogy of place for Black urban struggle. In A. Darder, M. Baltadano, & R. D. Torres (Eds.), *The critical pedagogy reader* (pp. 211-237). New York: Routledge Falmer.

Hempenstall, K. (2005). The whole language-phonics controversy: A historical perspective. *Australian Journal of Learning Difficulties*, 10(3), 19-33.

Hess, F. M. (1999). *Spinning Wheels: The Politics of Urban School Reform*. Washington, DC: Brookings Press.

Hill, P. T. & Celio, M. B. (1998). *Fixing urban schools*. Washington, DC: Brookings Institution Press.

Hirschland, M. J., & Steinmo, S. (2003). Correcting the record: Understanding the history of federal intervention and failure in securing U.S. educational reform. *Educational Policy*, 17(3), 343-364.

Huberman, M. (1993). The model of the independent artisan in teachers' professional relations. In. J. W. Little & M. W. McLauglin (Eds.), *Teachers' work: Individuals, colleagues and contexts*. (pp. 11-50). New York: Teachers College Press.

Ingersoll, R. M., & Smith, T. M. (2003). Do teacher induction and mentoring matter? *NASSP Bulletin*, 88(238), 28-40.

Johnson, S. M., Berg, J. H., & Donaldson, M. L. (2005). *Who stays in teaching and why? A review of the literature on teacher retention*. Cambridge, MA, Harvard Graduate School of Education: The Project on the Next Generation Teachers.

Jones, D. R. & Malen, B. (2002). Sources of victory, seeds of defeat: Linking enactment politics and implementation developments. In W. Hoy & C. Miskel (Eds.), *Theory and research in educational administration*, Volume 1 (pp. 41-76). Greenwich, CT: Information Age Publishing.

Knapp, M. S., Copland, M. A., & Talbert, J. E. (2003). *Leading for learning: Reflective tools for school and district leaders*. Seattle, WA: Center for the Study of Teaching and Policy.

Knight, T. (2003). Academic access and the family. In P. Kluth, D. M. Straut, and D. P. Biklen (Eds.), *Access to academics for all students: Critical approaches to Inclusive curriculum, instruction, and policy* (pp. 49-78). Mahwah, NJ: Lawrence Erlbuam Associates.

Kober, N. (2006). *A public education primer: Basic (and sometimes surprising) facts about the U.S. education system* (pp. 3-20). Retrieved November 1, 2007 from http://www.des.emory.edu/mfp/302/302PublicEducationPrimer.pdf.

Kosters, M. H. & Mast, B. D. (2003). *Closing the education achievement gap: Is Title I working?* Washington, DC: The AEI Press.

Kozol, J. (1991). *Savage inequalities: Children in America's schools*. New York: Harper Perennial.

———. (2005). *The shame of the nation: The restoration of apartheid schooling in America*. New York: Crown Publishing.

Ladson-Billings, G. (2006). *From the achievement gap to the educational dept: Understanding achievement in U.S. Schools*. Educational Researcher, 35(7), 3-12.

Lakoff, G. (2002). *Moral politics: How liberals and conservatives think.* Chicago, IL: The University of Chicago Press.

Lawson, M. A. (2003). School-family relationships in context: Parent and teacher perceptions of parent involvement. *Urban Educator,* 38(1), 77-133.

Lieberman, A. (1996). Practices that support teacher development: Transforming conceptions of professional learning. In M.W. McLaughlin & I. Oberman (Eds.), *Teacher learning: New policies, new practices.* New York: Teachers College Press.

Lipman, P. (1998). *Race, class, and power in school restructuring.* New York: SUNY Press.

Little, J. W. (2001). Professional development in pursuit of school reform. In A. Lieberman & L. Miller (Eds.), *Teachers caught in the action: Professional development that matters.* New York: Teachers College Press.

Lodge, C. & Reed, J. (2003). Transforming school improvement now and for the future. *Journal of Educational Change,* 4(1), 45-62.

Lytle, J. H. (2002). Whole-school reform from the inside. *Phi Delta Kappan,* 84(2), 164-167).

Malen, B., Croninger, R., Muncey, D., & Redmond-Jones, D. (2002). Reconstituting schools: "Testing" the "theory of action." *Educational Evaluation and Policy Analysis,* 24(2), 113-132.

Malen, B., Croninger, R., Redmond, D., & Muncey, D. (1999, October). *Uncovering the potential contradictions in reconstitution reforms.* Paper presented at the annual conference on the University Council for Educational Administration, Minneapolis, MN.

Manning, M. & Kamii, C. (2000). Whole language vs. isolated phonics instruction: A longitudinal study in kindergarten with reading and writing tasks. *Journal of Research in Childhood Education,* 15(1), 53-65.

Mathews, D. (1996). *Is there a public for public schools?* Dayton, OH: Kettering Foundation Press.

McLaughlin, M. W. (1993). What matters most in teachers' work context? In J. W. Little & M. W. McLauglin (Eds.), *Teachers work: Individuals, colleagues, and contexts,* (pp. 79-103). New York: Teachers College Press.

Meier, D. (2002). *In schools we trust: Creating communities of learning in an era of testing and standardization.* Boston: Beacon Press.

Metz, M. H. (1993). Teachers' ultimate dependence on their students. In J. W. Little & M. W. McLaughlin (Eds.), *Teachers' work: Individuals, colleagues, and contexts,* (pp. 104-136). New York: Teachers College Press.

Miles, M. B. (1964). Educational innovation the nature of the problem. In M. B. Matthew (Ed.), *Innovation in Education.* New York, NY: Teachers College Press.

National Commission on Excellence in Education. (1983). *A nation at risk: The imperative for educational reform.* Washington, DC: U.S. Department of Education.

National Center for Education Statistics (1996). *Urban schools: The challenge of location and poverty.* Washington, DC: Author.

National Education Association. (2003). *Status of the American Public School Teacher, 2001-2002.* Washington, DC: Author.

National Education Association. (November, 1998). Reconstituting low-performing schools, and the role of the union. In *Trends: Issues in Urban Education.* Retrieved January 15, 2003, from http://www.nea.org/bt/3-school/trnd1198.pdf.

Natriello, G. & Zumwaltz, K. (2003). New teachers for urban schools: The contribution of the provisional teacher program in New Jersey. *Education and Urban Society*, 23(1), 49-62.

Newmann, F. M., King, M. B., & Youngs, P. (2001). Professional development that addresses school capacity: Lessons from urban elementary schools. *American Journal of Education*, 108(4), 259-299.

Nieto, S. (1997). School reform and student achievement: A multicultural perspective. In J. A. Banks, and C. A. M. Banks (Eds.), *Multicultural Education: Issues and Perspectives* (pp. 387-407). Needham Heights, MA: Allyn and Bacon.

Noddings, N. (1992). *The challenge to care in schools: An alternative approach to education*. New York: Teachers College Press.

Noguera, P. A. (2003). *City schools and the American dream: Reclaiming the promise of public schools*. New York: Teachers College Press.

———. (2003b). The trouble with Black boys: The role and influence of environment and cultural factors on the academic performance of African American males. *Urban Education*, 38(4), 431-459.

Nonaka, I. & Takeuchi, H. (1995). *The knowledge creating company: How Japanese companies create the dynasties of innovation*. Oxford: Oxford University Press.

Orfield, G., & Eaton, S. (1996). *Dismantling desegregation*. New York: The New Press.

Orr, M. T. & Easley, J. II. (2009, April). *Searching for the core knowledge of educational leadership preparation and the effects of district influence: A comparison of two districts' initiative*. Paper presented at the Annual American Educational Research Association Meeting. San Diego, CA.

Polyni, M. (1958). *Personal knowledge: Towards a post-critical philosophy*. Chicago: University of Chicago Press.

———. (1966). *The tacit dimension*. New York: Doubleday.

Prestine, N. A. & McGreal, T. L. (1997). Fragile changes, sturdy lives: Implementing authentic assessment in schools. *Educational Administration Quarterly*, 33 (3), 371-400.

Ramirez, M. III. (1991). *Psychotherapy and counseling with minorities*. New York: Pergamon Press.

Rait, E. (1995). Against the current: Organizational learning in schools. In S. B. Bacharach & B. Mundell (Eds.), *Images of schools: structures and roles in organizational behavior* (pp. 71-107). Thousand Oaks, CA: Corwin Press.

Resnick, L. B. & Hall, M. W. (1998). Learning organizations for sustainable education reform. *Daedalus*, 127(4), 89-118.

Rice, J. K., & Croninger, R. G. (2001). *Resource generation, reallocation or depletion: A multidisciplinary analysis of the impact of school reconstitution on local capacity*. Paper presented at the Annual Conference of the American Finance Association, Cincinnati, OH.

Rice, J. K., & Malen, B. (2002, March). *The human costs of educational reform: The case of school reconstitution*. Paper presented at the Annual Conference on the American Education Finance Association, Albuquerque, NM.

Robertson, S. L. (1996). Teachers' work, restructuring and Postfordism: Constructing the new 'professionalism.' In I. F. Goodson & A. Hargreaves (Eds.), *Teachers' professional lives*, (pp. 28-55). London: Falmer Press.

Robinson, J. E., & Heinen, J. R., K. (1975). Some implications of cognitive styles for the teaching-learning process. *Education Research Methods*, 7(4), 87.

Rosenholtz, S. J. (1991). *Teachers' workplace: The social organization of schools*. New York: Teachers College Press.

Rowan, B. (1995). The organizational design of schools. In S. B. Bacharach & B. Mundell (Eds.), *Images of schools: structures and roles in organizational behavior* (pp. 11-42). Thousand Oaks, CA: Corwin Press.

Sarason, S. (1990). *The predictable failure of educational reform: Can we change course before it's too late?* San Francisco: Jossey-Bass.

Senge, P. M. (1990). *The fifth discipline: The art and practice of the learning organization*. New York: Currency Doubleday.

Sergiovanni, T. J. (1997). How can we move toward a community theory of supervision? Wrong theory/wrong practice. In J. Glanz & R. F. Newville (Eds.), *Educational Supervision: Perspectives Issues, and Controversies*. Massachusetts: Chirstopher-Gordon Publishers.

Smith-Maddox, R. (1998). Defining culture as a dimension of academic achievement: Implications for culturally responsive curriculum, instruction, and assessment. *The Journal of Negro Education, 67*(3), 302-317.

Smyth, J. (1991). *Teachers as collaborative learners: Challenging dominate forms of supervision*. Philadelphia: Open University Press.

Stage, E. K. (2005). Why do we need these assessments? *Natural Selection: Journal of the BSCS,* 11–13.

Thompson, G. L. (2003). Predicting African American parents' and guardians' satisfaction with teachers and public schools. *The Journal of educational Research, 96*(1), 277-285.

Tyack, D., & Tobin, W. (1994). The "grammar" of schooling: Why has it been so hard to change? *American Educational Research Journal,* 31(3), pp. 481-518.

U.S. Department of Education. (2001). *Family involvement in children's education: An idea book* (abridged version). Jessup, MD: Office of Educational Research and Improvement.

U.S. Department of Education. (2002, August). *Guidance on comprehensive school reform program*. Retrieved November 20, 2002, from http://www.ed.gov/offices/OESE/compreform/guidance2002.html

U.S. Department of Education. (2002b). *Meeting the high quality teacher's challenge: The Secretary's annual report on teacher quality*. Washington, DC: Author.

U.S. Department of Education. (1998, April). *Tools for schools: Introduction*. Retrieved November 20, 2002, from http://www.ed.gov/pubs/ToolsforSchools/intro.html.

Wegner, E. (1998). *Communities of practice: Learning, meaning and identity*. United Kingdom: Cambridge Press.

Wegner, E., McDormott, R., & Snyder, W. M. (2002). *Cultivating communities of practice*. Boston: Harvard Business School Press.

Wideen, M. F., Mayer-Smith, J. A., & Moon, B. J. (1996). Knowledge, teacher development and change. In I. F. Goodson & A. Hargreaves (Eds.), *Teachers' professional lives, (pp.187-204)*. London: Falmer Press.

Willie, R. & Howey, K. R. (1980). Reflections on adult development: Implications for inservice teacher education. In R.W. Houston (Ed.), *Staff development and educational change*. Reston, VA: Association of Teacher Educators.

Wilson, B. L. & Corbett, H. K. (2001). *Listening to urban kids: School reform and the teachers they want*. New York: SUNY.

Wilson, K. R. & Allen, W. R. (1987). Explaining the educational attainment of young Black adults: Critical familial and extra-familial influences. *Journal of Negro Education, 56*(1), 64-76.

Index

About the Author

Jacob Easley II is an associate professor in the School of Education at Mercy College, where he teachers various courses in educational leadership and urban education. *The Audacity to Teach!* is based on his dissertation research seeking to understand the impact of school reform on the teaching and learning processes. His work has been published in the *Journal of Educational Administration, Urban Education and Society,* and *Improving Schools.* Dr. Easley received his PhD from The Pennsylvania State University where he studied educational leadership and curriculum and supervision. Dr. Easley has served as a Martin Luther King, Jr. Scholar with the U.S. Department of Education. He is a leader in a member of professional organizations including the American Educational Research Association, the National Association of Holmes Scholars Alumni (President), and the Metropolitan Council of Education Administration Programs (Vice President) in New York City.